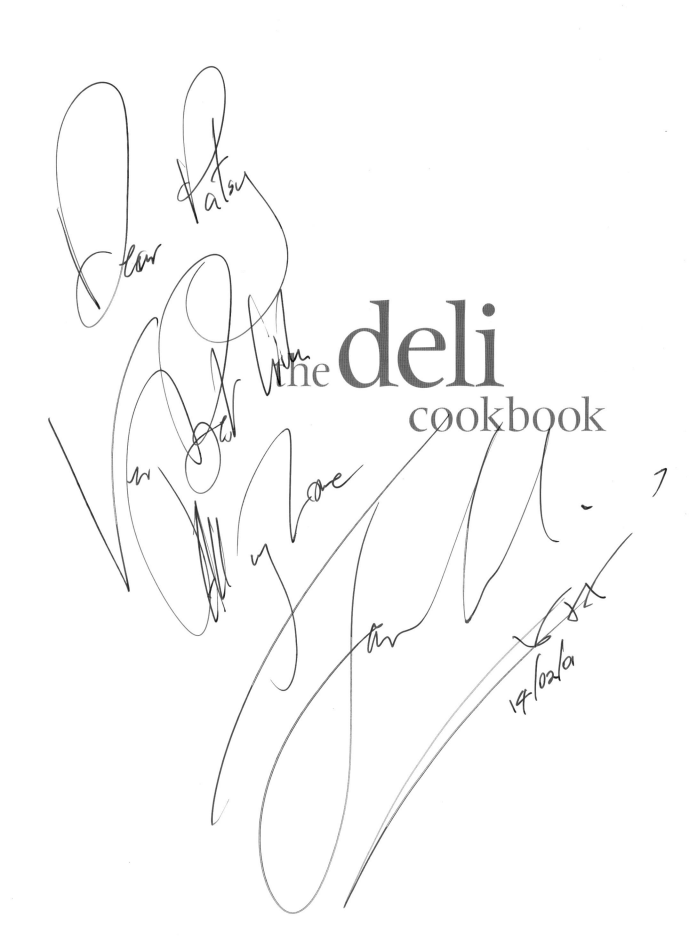

the deli
cookbook

the deli

cookbook

james martin

the deli cookbook

by james martin

First published in Great Britain in 2000 by
Mitchell Beazley, an imprint of Octopus Publishing
Group Limited, 2–4 Heron Quays, London E14 4JP.

A CIP catalogue record for this book is available from the British Library.

ISBN: 1 84000 211 5

The author and publishers will be grateful for any information which will assist
them in keeping future editions up to date. Although all reasonable care has
been taken in the preparation of this book, neither the publishers nor the author
can accept any liability for any consequences arising from the use thereof, or
the information contained therein.

Commissioning editors: Margaret Little, Rebecca Spry
Executive art editor: Tracy Killick
Photographer: William Reavell
Managing editor: Hilary Lumsden
Design: Nigel Soper, Colin Wheatland
Editor: Jo Richardson
Stylist: Liz Hippisley
Home economist: Katherine Ibbs, Nicola Fowler
Production: Jessame Emms
Index: Hilary Bird

Typeset in Helvetica

Printed and bound by Toppan Printing Company in China

Dedication Dear gran, although you are no longer here, I will always be
thinking of you.

Acknowledgements Firstly I would like to thank my agents Linda and Fiona for
all their nagging on the phone, you're both true stars. And to everyone at Mitchell
Beazley for all their support and to Ros Denny for all the nagging for recipes. To
my close friends and family for drinking me out of house and home. And finally to
everybody who has helped me, past and present, cheers to you all. And Erica for
sorting out my life first and paperwork second!

Contents

Introduction   6

Starters   12

Griddled asparagus with roasted red peppers   14
Chilli garlic dressed mushrooms   16
Chargrilled vegetables with olives and goats' cheese   16
Hot onion bread with garlic and hand-peeled tomatoes   17
Marinated mozzarella with red onion and spinach   17
Poppy seed snaps   18
Salad of roasted peppers and olives   18
Picos blue and caramelized onion tarts   20
Brandade of salt cod   21
Thai prawn and noodle soup   23
Scallop salad with salted capers and crispy sage   24
Salad of two smoked fish   25
Basil oil tuna with deep-fried garlic   27
Lobster, mango and rocket tarts   28
Potato, truffle and parma ham terrine   30
Gedi goats' cheese bruschetta with quince and parma ham   31
Figs roasted with blue cheese and proscuitto   32
Iberico ham with a herby leaf salad   34
Crispy speck, artichoke and black pudding salad   35
Bruschetta of smoked beef and melted brie   36
Bresaola with confit lemon rind and rocket salad   37

Main courses   38

Sea bass with summer herbs and roasted limes   40
Sea bass with pinenuts, artichokes and tomatoes   42
Sea bass with sprouting wheatgerm salad   43
Pepper-crusted monkfish with mustard dill sauce   45
Seared tuna with quinoa and kalamata olives   46
Turbot with boudin and black-eye beans   47
Salmon with red onion pickle   48

Salmon with wild garlic sauce and champ   50
Brill with Chinese lardons and green leaves   51
Halibut parcels with capers and pernod   52
Halibut steaks with beansprout and coriander salad   54
Pan-fried cod with vanilla shrimp butter   55
Cheats' coq au vin   56
Pan-fried chicken with chilli beans, fennel and pancetta   58
Duck breasts with fennel pâté and apples   59
Honeyed duck confit with crispy seaweed and creamy mash   61
Loins of lamb with cumin and almond-dressed artichokes   62
Anchovy and garlic-studded roast lamb   63
Roast pork with balsamic butter bean broth   64
Calves liver with port-flavoured pan juices   66
Beef steaks with sun-blushed tomatoes and parsley   67
Caramelized braised beef   69

Dishes on the side   70

Celeriac remoulade   72
Roast celeriac with vanilla and garlic   72
Caramelized beetroot   74
New potato salad with truffle cream dressing   74
Butter bean and rosemary purée   75
Olive focaccia with rosemary oil   76
Roasted garlic and olive oil bread   78
Roast butternut squash with lemon and mustard   79
Fresh leaf pasta   81
Bubble and squeak cakes   82
Smoked salmon and basil bread   83

One courses meals   84

Red onion and créme fraîche pizzas   86
Aubergine and mozzarella stacks   87
Anchovy and rosemary pizzas   88
Grilled gravadlax with pesto gnocchi   88
Mussel and artichoke risotto   90
Mullet on smoky red pepper salad   91
Seafood pot   93
Crab cakes   94
Leek and haddock risotto   95

Lemon-dressed pasta with chargrilled salmon   96
Charred smoked halibut and saffron risotto   98
Tortellini in a cèpes sauce   99
Chicken, flageolet and fennel salad   101
Chicken breasts with asparagus and muscat risotto   102
Penne carbonara   103
Pesto pasta with picante chorizo and artichokes   104

Puddings and cakes   106

Super-light pancakes   108
Chocolate and ginger cheesecake   110
Hot walnut tart   111
Warm banana tarte tatin   112
Hot chocolate fondants   114
Tiramisu   115
Basil-scented summer fruit terrine with lime syrup   117
Saffron and honey pears   118
Brandied roast figs   119
Vanilla ice-cream with crushed meringues   121
Honey mocha mousse   122
Homemade florentines   123
Panna cotta   124
Spiced oranges   126
Pineapple and polenta cakes with two coulis   127
Dripping cake   129
Quince and apple tarts with honey-walnut cream   130
Spiced pear and apple danish   131

Chutneys and preserves   132

Plum chutney   134
Muscat and vanilla syrup   136
Citrus and vanilla dressing   136
Cucumber and green pepper relish   137
Chicory and orange jam   139

Menu combinations   140
Recipe combinations   141
Index   142

Introduction

I delight in being a deli owner. There are so many aspects to the occupation that bring me such pleasure. The first is obviously food. The second is the direct contact I have with my customers – even the most novice of cooks has a valid opinion to offer. Selling direct to a wide range of food-lovers keeps me critically aware of what is or is not good food.

Food retailing nowadays is a highly technical and organized business. But a delicatessen is staffed by food-loving enthusiasts, like me and my ever faithful manager, Nick. I am more than happy to stock items from small independent producers and love trying out new cheeses and cold meats. Not for me market research surveys or profit

margins; I operate on the basis of gut reaction and look for natural taste and freshness. In fact, I only stock varieties or brands of produce that cannot be found in supermarkets – once a particular item becomes too popular, I move on to a new one. My store is a microcosm of good food on sale.

The recipes presented in this book all feature foods and ingredients that you can buy from a reputable deli. Certain items are common to many of the recipes, such as oils, vinegars, cheeses and flours; others are particular specialities that I have sourced or noted on my travels. Some of them have to be bought specially for the recipe, while others are used in small amounts yet will keep for the same, or many other, creative uses in the future. Many of the recipes will introduce you to a new ingredient and therefore a new taste, but there is no need to rush out and buy lots of different sauces or seasonings. Treat yourself to a new item, say, once a week, so that in just a few weeks you will have assembled a versatile collection of exciting, novel flavours that you can use at will to liven up even the simplest dish.

The recipes are generally quite simple to follow and recreate, but a few would suit the 'hobby' cook who loves to spend time in the kitchen. In the main they feed four people, but some are just for two, while others have been specially developed for entertaining on a grander scale. However, if the given number of servings doesn't suit your purpose or occasion, the recipes are flexible enough for you simply to multiply the ingredients up or reduce them down.

At the back of the book, you will find that I have combined recipes to create a selection of menus, which you might find helpful should you wish to push the boat out. But if time is short or you want to keep things simple, bear in mind that there is nothing more guaranteed to please than a platter of top-quality cold sliced charcuterie meats with olives and gherkins to start or a small a selection of choice cheeses for a dessert. There's no need to spend time in the kitchen to impress your guests.

You will find an almost bewildering array of produce on offer at the deli counter, so here is a guide to what I consider to be the essentials, with my personal recommendations for what to choose and sample.

Cheese

A good deli will have a comprehensive and adventurous choice of cheeses, all beautifully laid out and clearly labelled. Not only will there be a collection of the familiar, useful hard cheeses, such as cheddars and parmesan, but also some more unusual, exciting ones.

Cheeses for cooking tend to be the hard, matured types. A good montgomery or Canadian (unpasteurized) cheddar, at least one year old, will make a fantastic soufflé or sauce for macaroni cheese as well as being excellent to eat as it comes. In the case of parmesan, look for the genuine article which will be marked with a ring of red dots on the rind bearing the words 'parmigiano reggiano', indicating that it comes from a clearly defined area in Italy and has been made in the traditional way and matured for at least 18 months. Real parmesan will smell faintly milky and sweet and is quite crumbly in texture. Buy it in a small piece to grate yourself – not too much as it should be fresh – but please, never opt for the dried variety in a packet or drum. You can also shave parmesan with a swivel peeler and use the wafer-thin slices as a garnish for salads, as well as in pasta and risotto dishes.

You might also like to try Italian ewes' milk cheeses, sold under the collective name of pecorino. Mozzarella is another big favourite, made from curds heated in whey, which are then kneaded and stretched or rolled into balls. In Italy, mozzarella is sold fresh at a day old. I sell buffalo milk mozzarella (packed in buffalo milk rather than water) because it has the creamiest flavour and finest texture. Mascarpone is a thick Italian cream cheese, which is made by heating milk, then collecting the cream from the top and treating it with a culture (the rest of the milk is used to make parmesan). Ricotta is made by boiling whey used in making other cheeses, such as mozzarella. Soft curds form on the top, which are then scooped off, drained and chilled. Goats' cheese is increasingly popular with its characteristic tang and sweet, spicy aroma. Soft goats' cheeses are highly versatile, for sweet and savoury, while semi-soft chèvres and crottins are great for grilling.

Salamis and cold meats

The best salamis and cold meats have to come from a good deli, where they are freshly cut into wafer-thin slices in front of you. Ready-sliced salamis pressed into vacuum packs

generally taste greasy. Salamis are made from uncooked meat that is smoked (or air-dried) or pickled in brine, or both. The best salamis are rolled in edible, natural casings, but some are sold in plastic; peel both varieties before serving. Salamis range in texture from coarse and chunky through to fine and smooth. They also have different levels of saltiness and pungency, from the mild milano to the piquant napoletano. Added flavourings include fennel, paprika, chilli, black pepper and of course garlic. Fat is an integral part of a good salami and enhances the flavour.

Raw and cured hams are the large leg joints we see hanging up in delis, or clamped on a ham stand awaiting the long, thin slicing knife or machine; as with salamis, they are best thinly sliced on the spot. The best known is prosciutto di parma or parma ham which comes from a clearly defined region around Parma. These hams carry a gold ducal crown on their rind. Parma pigs are a special pampered breed which is fed on grain and the whey from making parmesan. This special diet, and the hanging of the hams in rooms with open windows, give the hams their special flavour. Other quality hams to try include Spanish iberico ham (*see* the recipe on page 34), made from black-hoofed pigs fed on acorns. French cured hams include popular bayonne ham. Don't trim the fat off these hams – it's part of the taste sensation.

Italian or Spanish speck is my favourite bacon for cooking; the Poles and other middle Europeans have their own types of speck. This meat is traditionally quite fatty, with a sweet, smoky flavour. Sold generally in one piece, you can have it thinly sliced. Pancetta is smoked streaky bacon from Italy, which cooks to a delicious crispness. You can either buy it in a roll or a streaky slab, but always have it sliced wafer-thin, otherwise it can be chewy.

Blood sausages are a great favourite of mine – especially traditional British black pudding, which is ruby-red, speckled with chunks of creamy fat, with a sweet, spicy smell. Always fry black pudding over a high heat to get a good crispness to the outside. Boudin (blanc and noir) are French blood sausages used to add flavour to casseroles. Morcilla and botifarra are blood pork sausages from Spain, sometimes flavoured with cinnamon, and can be used in the same way as boudin. Chorizos are Spanish pork sausages that have been spiced, marinated and then cured. They are aromatic and gutsy, flavoured with red pepper, paprika and/or chilli and garlic. There

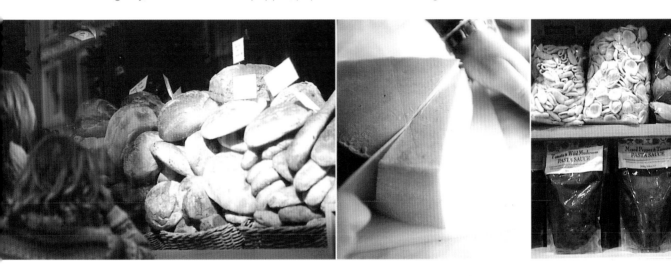

are over 50 types of chorizo – the fully cured varieties are long and thin like church candles; the semi-cured are thicker and good for grilling or casseroling.

Oils

Olive oils vary in colour from pale yellow through to cloudy green, depending on the country of origin and the production method. Oil is extracted from olives at differing stages, and one olive can go through several pressings. The first pressing gives the lightest and best quality oil, known as extra virgin olive oil. Since the olives are not subject to any heat treatment, the pressing is known as 'cold pressing'. This oil has the most character and flavour. It may sometimes have a little sediment or look slightly cloudy, but the quality will still be good. The second pressing, with or without heating the olives, yields pure olive oil, sometimes known as 'virgin oil'. It is not as full flavoured or pungent as extra virgin olive oil, but it is still relatively expensive and slightly heavy. Nevertheless, it is an excellent all-purpose oil, suitable for use in many dishes. I like my oil quite peppery in flavour, a sensation you will notice on the back of your throat when you sip it neat.

Check the labels of olive oil bottles carefully, because the oils may not be quite as they seem. Most olive oil in Europe comes from Spain, but it can be bottled in another country, such as Italy. Therefore, the oil may be made from Spanish olives but bottled in

Tuscany. Many oils are from single producers and this, too, will be noted on the label; my favourite is Azienda Agrocola from the Possenti Castelui Estate in Umbria. Organic oils have a good flavour and quality. Avoid oils with fancy labels – a good oil will often be in a plain bottle. If you want to sample an oil without sipping it, rub a little between your palms and inhale – the warmth of your hands will release the complex aromas.

Flavoured olive oils are becoming popular. Lemon olive oil is made by pressing lemon skins along with the olives and it tastes fragrantly citrusy. To make basil olive oil, basil leaves are steeped in the oil and then it is heat-treated to make it safe. Don't be tempted to make herb oils yourself unless you store the oil in the refrigerator and use it quickly. Walnut, almond, hazelnut, sesame and pistachio oils are great for using in small amounts to flavour dressings and salads, for tossing with hot pasta or new potatoes or for drizzling

over grilled fish. Groundnut oil is a good-quality frying oil, much favoured by Chinese cooks, who use it for high-temperature frying because it won't easily burn.

Vinegars

There is so much you can do with a good, fruity, acidic vinegar. The finer the flavour, the less you need to use. A good vinegar will come from a single source and have a fair amount of information about its origin, content and production on the label. Wine vinegar is the most useful. One of my favourites, called Forvm, is made from the Cabernet Sauvignon grape from Spain and is bursting with flavour. Sherry vinegar is full-flavoured, too, and delicious in robust salad dressings, it's also good for de-glazing pans after frying meats or fish. Rice wine vinegar is light and delicate – a classic ingredient in Oriental cooking and ideal for salad dressings.

Whole books have been devoted to the subject of balsamic vinegars, and these wonderful liquids are indeed in a class of their own. Balsamic vinegars have been made for hundreds of years around the Italian city of Modena. They are aged vinegars, left to mature in barrels and painstakingly transferred from one barrel to the next over time. Balsamic vinegars should be aged for at least one year, but some will have been matured for eight to 20 years – the label should give the age. The rarest and most expensive can be as much as 100 years old, tasting like the finest château wine. Some balsamic vinegars from California have been crushed with fruits – figs, cherries, blackcurrants etc. Consequently, the vinegar contains the juice and pulp of these fruits and has the consistency of a fruit coulis. It is excellent drizzled over ice-cream or fruits as well as grilled meats and fish.

Pickles, chutneys and dressings

This is where the small producer reigns supreme. My two favourite suppliers are the Bay Tree Food Company and Mary Berry (and daughter) Dressings, both have a fresh homemade flavour from natural ingredients and not just essences. A cracking sauce is Roaring Lady – a feisty little number made from sun-dried tomatoes, capers and

chillies. From my home county of Yorkshire herald wonderful pickled eggs, pickled shallots and chutneys from a small farm near Beverley, Yorkshire, including my favourite Yorkshire ketchup, which has a delicious smoky flavour. Brindisa Foods imports Mustard Fruits such as figs, tangerines and mixed fruits from Spain, which are great with cheese or salads.

Chocolate

Chocolate is a vast subject, but it helps to have a basic knowledge of quality. Chocolate is made from cocoa solids, cocoa butter, sugars, milk and even vegetable fats. The higher the percentage of cocoa solids, the finer the flavour and darker the colour of the chocolate. However, chocolate with a content of over 60 per cent cocoa solids can be a little tricky to melt, since it can seize and turn solid if overheated. Top chefs use chocolate that contains up to 75 per cent cocoa solids, but 50–60 per cent is the most practical for home cooks. If you want to increase the chocolate flavour, simply blend in some cocoa powder. Milk chocolate contains around 30–35 per cent cocoa solids. White chocolate has no dark cocoa mass – just cocoa butter, milk and sugar – but it can still have cocoa solids of around 35 per cent. The best brands for cooking are Valrhona, the Chocolate Society and Cocoa Barry. For delicious drinking chocolate, I recommend Charbonnel et Walker.

Starters

The Americans have the right idea when it comes to starters. They call them 'appetizers', and that sums up exactly what they should be about. First courses should create the mood for eating, prompt the gastric juices to flow and set the tone for the meal.

A good starter should look inviting, with colours that either grab the attention or are pleasingly harmonized. Both texture and flavour should delight your tongue and leave you wanting more, but neither should be so overpowering that they pulverize or anaesthetize your tastebuds, leaving them in an unfit state to savour what's to come.

The deli offers the perfect solution to preparing high-quality yet effortless starters, guaranteed to put even the most fussy eaters at ease, leaving them happy to relax and enjoy the rest of the meal as and when it comes. This selection of dishes features the stars of the chill cabinet – smoked fish, cheeses and cured meats – to create simple yet imaginative salads and cold platters or sophisticated hot savouries and funky finger foods. Other recipes major on storecupboard deli delights – jars of wonderfully smoky-flavoured chargrilled vegetables and the best, most delicious tomatoes you can buy – to make almost instant first courses or light meals.

Customer feedback is vital for me, I love seeing the pleasure on people's faces when I hand them a tasty morsel of something new and it keeps them coming back for more.

A simple early summer feast, ideal as a starter. I look forward to May when a local farmer from the Hampshire village of Chabolton supplies me with bundles of his superb green asparagus spears. He was one of my suppliers at the Hotel du Vin in Winchester, and would happily pick spears to order.

Griddled asparagus with roasted red peppers

2 bunches of fresh
green asparagus, about
500 g (1 lb 2 oz)

2 large red peppers,
halved lengthways,
cored and deseeded

a little olive oil,
for brushing

50 g (1¾ oz) unsalted
butter, melted

sea salt and freshly
ground black pepper

1 To prepare the asparagus spears, trim the bases and use a swivel vegetable peeler to shave the woody stems. Bring a large pan of salted water to the boil and have a large bowl of iced cold water at the ready.

2 Blanch the asparagus for 2–3 minutes in the boiling water, then drain and immediately drop into the bowl of iced water. This prevents any further cooking and maintains the colour.

3 While the asparagus is cooling, heat the oven to 200°C (400°F), Gas Mark 6. Place the peppers, cut side down, on a baking sheet and brush the skins with oil.

4 Roast the peppers in the oven for about 15 minutes or until the skins blacken and blister. Remove to a bowl and cover with clingfilm. Leave for 5 minutes, then peel off the skins.

5 Heat a griddle pan until you can feel a good heat rising. Place the asparagus spears on to the hot metal and allow to char slightly. Transfer to warmed serving plates and arrange in a spray pattern. Season well. Position the pepper halves at the base of the spears and drizzle over the melted butter.

Chilli garlic dressed mushrooms

This is a wow of a starter! We use this recipe in my deli, and customers buy the mushrooms either to serve as starters or, if smaller mushrooms are used, for tapas. Make sure you use a good-quality olive oil.

serves 4

8–12 field mushrooms, depending on size

100 ml (3½ fl oz) extra virgin olive oil

2 fat fresh garlic cloves, chopped

½ large fresh red chilli, deseeded and chopped

1 shallot, chopped

1 tbsp lemon juice

sea salt and freshly ground black pepper

1 Heat the grill until hot. Wipe the mushrooms clean, if necessary (do not wash them – it makes them slimy). Brush the tops and gills with about half the oil and season. Grill for about 3 minutes on each side until softened.

2 Meanwhile, whisk the remaining oil with the garlic, chilli, shallot, lemon juice and seasoning.

3 Place the mushrooms in a shallow serving dish, pour over the dressing and mix thoroughly. Leave until cooled to room temperature.

serving note

These mushrooms are lovely served with crusty bread to mop up the juices.

variation

You could make this dish with large button mushrooms in place of field mushrooms. Pan-fry in olive oil instead of grilling them.

Chargrilled vegetables with olives and goats' cheese

A selection of ready-chargrilled vegetables packed in oil makes a wonderful basis for a quick starter or light main course, tossed with olives, dressed with pesto and topped with goats' cheese. Serve with hunks of country bread. Don't let the remainder of the oil drained from the vegetables go to waste. Use it to make dressings for salads or to drizzle over hot new potatoes.

serves 4

3–4 x 300 g (10½ oz) jars chargrilled vegetables in oil, eg artichokes, courgettes, aubergines, peppers and mushrooms, drained but the oil reserved

2 tbsp black olives

4 tbsp freshly made pesto

2 tbsp balsamic vinegar

2 tbsp chopped fresh herbs, eg oregano, dill, basil or parsley

2–3 tbsp toasted pinenuts

175 g (6 oz) goats' cheese log

sea salt and freshly ground black pepper

1 Toss the chargrilled vegetables in a large bowl with the olives and seasoning, using plenty of pepper.

2 Mix the pesto with the vinegar and a little of the drained oil from the vegetables to taste. Add to the vegetables with the herbs and toss well. Divide between serving plates and scatter over the pinenuts.

3 Heat the grill until hot. Slice the goats' cheese into 4 rounds and grill on one side until bubbling, golden brown and soft in the centre. Lift from the grill rack using a palette knife and place on top of the vegetables. Serve immediately.

ingredients note

I use Spanish ingredients for this dish – olives from Aragon and montenebro cheese.

Hot onion bread with garlic and hand-peeled tomatoes

serves 4

1 loaf onion bread, thickly sliced

4–5 fat fresh garlic cloves, chopped

200 ml (7 fl oz) olive oil

about 8 large fresh basil leaves, roughly chopped or torn

400 g (14 oz) jar pomodoro sammarzano (hand-peeled tomatoes with basil in oil), drained but oil reserved (for use in dressings)

sea salt flakes (*see* ingredients notes, page 76) and freshly ground black pepper

Italian tomatoes have the best flavour without doubt, and some are worth paying a few pounds for, even though you may think twice about the cost compared to the canned variety. Pomodoro sammarzano are whole, hand-peeled tomatoes packed in jars with olive oil and fresh basil leaves. These are not tomatoes for cooking. I would advise you to eat them as 'neat' as possible, on wonderful hand-baked bread, such as the onion loaves from my favourite bakers, Degustibus, in Oxford. Walnut bread would work just as well. This is simple, rustic food that tastes fantastic.

1 Heat the grill until hot. Lay the bread slices on the grill rack. Whisk the garlic and oil together, then spoon over the bread, coating well.

2 Grill the bread until pale golden on both sides and divide between 4 serving plates. Scatter over the fresh basil.

3 Spoon the tomatoes on to each plate and crush sea salt flakes on top, then grind over the pepper. Let each diner squash his or her tomatoes on to the toasted bread.

Marinated mozzarella with red onion and spinach

serves 4

4 balls buffalo mozzarella, about 100 g (3½ oz) each

200 g (7 oz) crème fraîche (full- or half-fat)

2–3 tbsp extra virgin olive oil

1 garlic clove, chopped

2 tbsp chopped fresh herbs, eg parsley, basil, oregano or dill

1 tbsp balsamic vinegar

200 g (7 oz) baby leaf spinach

½ red onion, thinly sliced

sea salt and freshly ground black pepper

Crème fraîche makes a really good dressing, especially for smothering over sliced buffalo mozzarella. Use half-fat crème fraîche for a lighter sauce. The red onion and spinach add colour as well as flavour. I bet this becomes a popular starter.

1 Drain the mozzarella balls of milk (reserving the milk if using full-fat crème fraîche – *see* step 2), then cut each into 4–5 slices.

2 Whisk the crème fraîche with 1 tbsp of the oil, garlic, half the chopped herbs and seasoning. (If using full-fat crème fraîche, you may want to thin the dressing down a little with some of the mozzarella milk.)

3 Toss the mozzarella slices with the crème fraîche dressing and chill in the refrigerator for about 1 hour.

4 Meanwhile, whisk together the remaining oil, vinegar and seasoning. When ready to serve, toss the spinach with the onion in the vinegar dressing, then divide between 4 serving plates. Spoon the dressed cheese on top, season with pepper and scatter over the remaining herbs.

Poppy seed snaps

makes about 250 g (9 oz)

200 g (7 oz) bread flour, ideally Italian Tipo 2 (see ingredients note)
a good pinch of salt
100–150 ml (3½–5 fl oz) water
3 tbsp olive oil
50 g (1¾ oz) poppy seeds

The recipe bakes to a thin unleavened bread which you can break into jagged wafers for serving with pâtés, such as the Brandade of salt cod, page 21, or simply with a creamy cheese.

1 Mix the flour and salt with enough cold water to form a thick dough. You can do this in a food processor.
2 Pull off a lump of dough the size of a large walnut and feed it through the widest setting of a pasta rolling machine 3 or 4 times. Turn the machine to a thinner setting and feed the dough through again. Do this several times, turning the setting down 2 more stages as the dough gets smoother and more elastic, as if you were making pasta. Don't crank the machine too enthusiastically, or the dough might break.
3 Place the dough on a flat baking sheet, brush with oil and sprinkle generously with poppy seeds.
4 Repeat the process with the remaining dough, a lump at a time, until it is all used up.
5 Meanwhile, heat the oven to 190°C (375°F), Gas Mark 5. Bake the poppy seed-covered dough sheets in batches for about 10 minutes until golden brown. Slide on to a wire rack to cool. When completely cold and brittle, snap into biscuit-sized pieces. Store in airtight containers.

ingredients note

Alternatively, use strong bread flour or a mixture of half strong white and brown wheatmeal (not wholemeal) flour to imitate the texture and colour of the original, Italian Tipo 2.

Salad of roasted peppers and olives

serves 4

2 large red peppers, halved lengthways, cored and deseeded
2–3 tbsp good-quality, aged balsamic vinegar
1 tbsp chopped fresh oregano or marjoram, or 1 tsp dried
1 shallot, finely chopped
a small handful of black olives, pitted and roughly chopped
sea salt and whole black peppercorns

This dish goes well with a simple grill of steaks or fish. Alternatively, serve as part of tapas with the Brandade of salt cod, page 21.

1 Heat the oven to 200°C (400°F), Gas Mark 6. Place the peppers, cut side down, on a baking sheet. Roast for 15–20 minutes until the skins start to char. Remove from the baking sheet, cover with a clean tea towel and allow to cool. Peel off the skins – they should be fairly easy to remove, but it doesn't matter if a little remains.
2 Cut the peppers into strips and place in a serving bowl. Crack the whole black peppercorns with the flat side of a wide blade knife. Drizzle the vinegar over the peppers and stir in the herb, shallot, olives, salt and cracked peppercorns. Allow to cool before serving.

serving note

This salad is also good served with poppy seed grissini, which you can make by simply rolling breadsticks in crème fraîche, then tossing in poppy seeds. Eat them quite quickly, before they go soggy.

Picos blue is a creamy Spanish blue cheese that bakes beautifully as a tart filling. I like to team it with caramelized onions, which you can buy ready-made in the form of a relish or chutney. The best is produced by the Bay Tree Food Company. If you can, use a balsamic vinegar that is at least eight years old for the dressing. It will reward you with a more mellow flavour.

Picos blue and caramelized onion tarts

makes 4
individual tarts

500g (1lb 2oz) frozen puff
or shortcrust pastry,
thawed

250g (9oz) picos blue,
rind removed

90g (3¼oz) mascarpone

2 large egg yolks

leaves stripped from a
large sprig of fresh thyme

½ x 340g (11¾oz)
jar caramelized onion
relish or chutney

sea salt and freshly
ground black pepper

frilly salad leaves, to serve

dressing

90g (3¼oz) sun-dried
tomatoes in oil, drained
and finely chopped, plus
1 tbsp of the oil

1 tbsp chopped fresh dill

2 tbsp good-quality, aged
balsamic vinegar

2 tbsp extra virgin olive oil

1 small garlic clove,
crushed

1 small shallot, finely
chopped

1 Roll out the pastry on a lightly floured surface to the thickness of a £1 coin and cut out 4 x 13cm (5in) rounds. Use to line a 4-hole Yorkshire pudding tin or 4 individual tartlet tins about 10cm (4in) in diameter. Prick the bases all over with a fork and place in the refrigerator for about 20 minutes to rest. Heat the oven to 200°C (400°F), Gas Mark 6.

2 The tarts are best baked blind first. Line each pastry case with foil, add baking beans and set the tins on a metal baking sheet. Bake for 12–15 minutes, remove the foil and beans and return to the oven for a further 5 minutes if the pastry still looks a little raw.

3 Meanwhile, beat the blue cheese and mascarpone thoroughly until creamy, then mix in the egg yolks, thyme leaves, freshly ground pepper and a little salt.

4 Remove the tarts from the oven and reduce the heat to 180°C (350°F), Gas Mark 4. Spoon a scant tablespoon of relish or chutney into each tart base, then top with the cheese mixture. Return to the oven and bake for about 15 minutes until the filling is just set.

5 Meanwhile, to make the dressing, whisk the chopped tomatoes with the reserved oil, add the remaining ingredients and season to taste.

6 Place the tarts on small serving plates with an extra dollop of caramelized onion relish or chutney on the side. Drizzle the dressing around each tart, grind over some black pepper and add a leaf or two of frilly lettuce to serve.

Brandade of salt cod

Brandade is a homemade salt cod pâté popular in France, but it can be found in various other guises throughout the rest of the Mediterranean. Salt cod originates from Scandinavia and was one of the mainstays of the European diet for centuries. It was also exported to the West Indies during the dark days of slavery as a high-protein food and is still popular there. You need a good-quality salt cod that is thick and still a little pliable, rather than stiff and grey, from Spain or Portugal. Start preparing the dish 24 hours in advance.

serves 4

400 g (14 oz) thick-cut salt cod fillets

100 ml (3½ fl oz) olive oil

1 fat garlic clove, chopped

150 ml (¼ pt) double cream

2 tbsp cooked potato, mashed

a dribble of good-quality truffle oil (*see* ingredients note, page 99 – optional)

grated zest and juice of 1 lemon

freshly ground black pepper

1 Soak the salt cod in plenty of cold water 24 hours in advance, changing the water every 6 hours or thereabouts (according to your sleep pattern!). Drain thoroughly.

2 Place the soaked cod in a large pan of cold water and bring to the boil. Remove from the heat and leave the cod to steep in the water as it cools. By then it will have cooked. Drain, skin and flake the fish, checking for and discarding any bones. Transfer to a food processor or blender.

3 Gently heat the olive oil with the garlic in a small saucepan. In a separate small saucepan, gently heat the cream until hot, then add the mashed potato with a tiny amount of truffle oil, if using. Mix well.

4 With the food processor or blender running, add the creamy potato, then the garlicky oil and blend until you have a creamy, scoopable paste. Season with pepper (it won't need any salt). Add the lemon zest and juice to taste before spooning the brandade into a serving bowl.

serving note

This is great served as part of tapas with the Salad of roasted peppers and olives, page 18, and crusty, country-style bread.

Classic Thai soups often consist of clear broth poured into bowls, piled high with thin rice vermicelli noodles. This is a quick adaptation of a salmon and lobster soup that I occasionally make. Here, I've used fresh tiger prawns and added the shells to bought fresh fish stock to enrich its flavour and colour.

Thai prawn and noodle soup

serves 4

300 g (10½ oz) whole uncooked tiger prawns, thawed if frozen

1 tsp coriander seeds

2 cm (¾ in) piece fresh galangal or 1 cm (½ in) piece fresh root ginger, sliced (*see* ingredients notes)

800 ml (1 pt 7 fl oz) fresh fish stock (buy ready-made in a tub)

200 g (7 oz) thin rice or egg noodles (*see* ingredients notes)

3 tbsp Thai fish sauce

2 fat fresh red chillies, deseeded and thinly sliced

2–4 garlic cloves (to taste), thinly sliced

1 salmon fillet, about 200 g (7 oz), skinned and cut into small cubes

4 spring onions, chopped

1 tbsp chopped fresh coriander

1 tbsp chopped fresh mint

juice 1 lemon or 2 limes

a little sesame oil (optional)

sea salt and freshly ground black pepper

1 Peel and de-spine the prawns (as shown below), reserve the shells and set aside. Place the prawn shells, coriander seeds and galangal or ginger in a saucepan with the stock. Bring to the boil, then simmer gently for 5 minutes. Leave to stand for 10 minutes before straining. Return the strained stock to the pan.

2 Meanwhile, reconstitute the noodles according to the packet instructions. Drain and keep warm.

3 Bring the stock back to the boil and add the fish sauce, chillies and garlic. Reduce the heat and simmer for 2 minutes. Add the prawns to the pan with the salmon, and return to a simmer to cook gently for about 3 minutes, until both are firm and cooked. Add the onions, herbs and lemon or lime juice to taste.

4 Divide the noodles between soup bowls. Using a slotted spoon, lift out the prawns, fish and flavourings and place around the noodles. Season the hot stock and pour into the bowls. Drizzle over a little sesame oil, if liked.

ingredients notes

Galangal is available in most Asian food stores – it is similar to fresh root ginger, but milder. You can also buy the noodles from Asian food stores, although many supermarkets now sell a good selection.

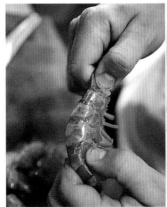

Scallop salad with salted capers and crispy sage

serves 4

12 fresh king scallops, prepared, with corals left on

200 g (7 oz) rocket leaves

100 g (3½ oz) watercress a large handful of fresh flat leaf parsley

sunflower oil, for deep-frying

8 large fresh sage leaves

1 tbsp olive oil

15 g (½ oz) butter

2–3 tbsp salted capers

sea salt and freshly ground black pepper

dressing

3 tbsp olive oil

juice of 1 large lemon

½ large fresh red chilli, deseeded and chopped

2 garlic cloves, chopped

sea salt and freshly ground black pepper

Fishmongers often sell lovely plump king scallops ready cleaned. They are rather pricey, but worth it for every deliciously sweet mouthful, and you only need about three per head for this salad. Salted capers, which are increasingly readily available in jars, add a feisty dimension to the green salad, and deep-fried sage leaves provide the final flourish.

1 Check that the scallops have been thoroughly cleaned and remove any thin black threads. Pat dry with kitchen paper and set aside.

2 Toss the rocket and watercress together in a large bowl. Remove the leaves from the parsley sprigs and add to the bowl.

3 Heat the sunflower oil to a depth of about 1 cm (½ in) in a shallow pan. When the oil is hot enough to detect a haze rising from it, add the sage leaves one at a time and deep-fry for 1 minute until just translucent. Drain on kitchen paper. Remember to turn off the heat under the oil pan as soon as you have finished, for safety's sake.

4 For the dressing, whisk the oil with the lemon juice, chilli, garlic and seasoning. Toss the salad leaves with the dressing, season and divide between 4 serving plates.

5 Heat a large non-stick frying pan until you feel a good heat rising. Add the olive oil, then the scallops and fry for about 2 minutes on each side, seasoning well. Do not overcook, or they will become tough. Add the butter and allow the scallops to soak up the buttery pan juices. Arrange on the salad and scatter over the capers. Grind over more pepper and serve immediately.

There are some excellent small local smokehouses now selling an impressive range of smoked fish. In our deli we sell products from a small firm in Fife, including traditional Arbroath smokies. This quick salad features smoked trout and eel with a creamy horseradish sauce, in perfect contrast to crisp bacon and bitter salad leaves. It is substantial enough to serve as a light meal.

serves 4

100 ml (3½ fl oz) fresh fish stock (buy ready-made in a tub)

2 tbsp horseradish sauce

225 g (8 oz) smoked streaky bacon, rinded

300 g (10½ oz) smoked trout fillets

300 g (10½ oz) smoked eel fillets

100 ml (3½ fl oz) double cream

about 200 g (7 oz) frisée lettuce or other bitter frilly leaves, rinsed in very cold water, drained and torn into pieces

4 tbsp chopped fresh parsley

2 tbsp chopped fresh chives

extra virgin olive oil

sea salt and freshly ground black pepper

Salad of two smoked fish

1 Heat the stock in a saucepan until boiling and continue to boil, uncovered, until reduced by half. Leave to cool a little. Place the horseradish sauce in a bowl and beat in the reduced stock to form a purée. Set aside to cool.

2 Heat the grill until hot. Grill the bacon rashers until crisp, then drain on kitchen paper. When cool enough to handle, break into bite-sized pieces. Break the fish into bite-sized flakes.

3 Whip the cream until softly stiff, then fold into the horseradish purée. Place the salad leaves in a large bowl with the parsley, and toss with about half the horseradish dressing and a little seasoning.

4 Divide the salad mixture between serving plates. Arrange the fish and bacon on top, spoon over the remainder of the dressing, then sprinkle over the chives. Drizzle each serving with a little olive oil and serve immediately.

serving note

This salad is best served with slices of a light rye bread.

Californian chefs have evolved a unique style by simply not imposing any constraints on their cooking. Consequently, they excel at mixing and matching the very best of every cuisine. This recipe is based on a dish I ate in the buzzy Napa Valley restaurant of chef Michael Chiarello called Tra Vigne. With over 250 covers for lunch and dinner and a real wood-burning oven at the heart of the restaurant, the atmosphere was really jumpin'. You'll need a very fresh loin of tuna for this recipe since it is served raw, sliced wafer thin.

Basil oil tuna with deep-fried garlic

serves 4

a long fillet of tuna loin, about 350 g (12 oz) (*see* ingredients notes)

5 tbsp basil oil (see ingredients notes)

2 large lemons

groundnut oil, for frying

5 fat garlic cloves, sliced wafer thin

3 shallots, sliced wafer thin

100 g (3½ oz) rocket leaves

sea salt and freshly ground black pepper

1 Trim the tuna to form a neat log shape and wrap tightly in clingfilm. Place in the freezer for about 1 hour until firm. This makes for easier slicing.

2 Slice the ice-cold tuna as thinly as possible and lay out on 4 serving plates, as you would slices of smoked salmon. Brush all over with half the basil oil, season and place in the refrigerator for 30 minutes to absorb the flavour.

3 Meanwhile, peel one of the lemons and remove the white pith. Cut between the membranes to remove the segments. Squeeze the juice from the other lemon. Set the segments and juice aside.

4 Heat the groundnut oil to a depth of 3 cm (1¼ in) in a frying pan. When hot but not smoking, add the garlic and shallots and deep-fry for 1–2 minutes until pale golden

brown and crisp. Drain on kitchen paper and set aside.

5 Dress the rocket leaves with the remaining basil oil, then toss with the lemon juice and seasoning.

6 Place the dressed rocket leaves and lemon segments on the edge of each plate of tuna, then scatter over the crispy garlic and shallots. Serve immediately.

ingredients notes

Use yellowfin tuna for the best flavour. For the dressing, I use Consozio Basil Oil as made by Chef Chiarello himself.

serving note

Thinly sliced rye bread makes an excellent accompaniment for this dish.

Lobster, mango and rocket tarts

This is a really glamorous starter yet deceptively easy to make; the pastry cases are quickly made from ready-to-use filo pastry (you will find a 4-hole Yorkshire pudding tin useful here). Make sure that everything is prepared and waiting to be assembled just before serving.

serves 4

4–6 large sheets of filo pastry, thawed if frozen (*see* ingredients note)

about 50 g (1¾ oz) butter, melted

1 whole cooked lobster, about 500 g (1 lb 2 oz)

1 large mango, ripe but not soft

4 tbsp Citrus and vanilla dressing (*see* page 136)

1 tbsp olive oil

2 tsp balsamic vinegar

about 100 g (3½ oz) rocket leaves

4 large fresh basil leaves, finely chopped

sea salt and freshly ground black pepper

1 Cut the filo pastry into 20 x 15 cm (6 in) squares. Keep the cut squares under a clean tea towel to prevent them drying out too quickly.

2 Brush each square quickly and lightly with the melted butter and place one in each hole of a 4-hole Yorkshire pudding tin or 4 individual tartlet tins about 10 cm (4 in) in diameter. Add 4 more squares, one at a time, to each hole or tin, placing each square at a slightly different angle to the one before, to form a crown shape. Make sure that the pastry is well pressed into the sides of the holes or tins. Chill in the refrigerator until ready to bake.

3 Heat the oven to 180°C (350°F), Gas Mark 4. Crack the shell of the lobster and extract the cooked flesh from the tail and claws. Cut into neat pieces.

4 Place the lobster meat on a non-stick baking sheet. Peel the mango thinly and cut the flesh into long neat slices. Place on the

baking sheet with the lobster and brush with half the Citrus and vanilla dressing. Set aside

5 Bake the filo pastry cases in the oven for about 10–12 minutes until crisp and lightly golden. Allow to cool before carefully lifting from the tins and transferring to a wire rack to cool completely.

6 Meanwhile, whisk the oil with the vinegar. Add to the rocket leaves with the seasoning and toss well. Place the mango and lobster in the oven to heat through for about 5 minutes.

7 Fill the tarts with the mango, lobster, rocket and basil. Drizzle over the remainder of the Citrus and vanilla dressing, season and serve immediately.

ingredients note

For the filo pastry, choose a good-quality Greek brand, such as Pittas.

Potato, truffle and parma ham terrine

serves 6

650 g (1 lb 7oz) firm potatoes, preferably maris piper or desirée

about 12 slices parma ham

150 g (5½ oz) butter, melted

50 g (1¾ oz) sliced black truffles (optional but memorable)

2 tbsp chopped fresh chives

sea salt and freshly ground black pepper

dressing

1 tbsp finely chopped black truffle (optional)

2 plum tomatoes, deseeded and finely chopped

3 tbsp balsamic vinegar

grated zest and juice of 1 lemon

100 ml (3½ fl oz) olive oil

1 tbsp chopped fresh parsley

Despite the luxurious nature of this starter, it doesn't take long to put together. However, you need to assemble the terrine the night before so that it can be pressed overnight in the refrigerator. Buy the parma ham freshly sliced and laid out neatly on waxed paper, to prevent the slices from sticking together. Truffle slices are available packed in oil – you can use some of the oil for the dressing.

1 Boil the potatoes in their skins in a saucepan of lightly salted water for about 15 minutes until tender. Drain and leave to cool a little. Peel while still lukewarm, then cut into 1 cm (½ in) slices.

2 Line a 450 g (1 lb) terrine mould or loaf tin with clingfilm, pressing it into the sides firmly and smoothly. Line the mould or tin with half the slices of parma ham, allowing the ends of the slices to hang over the sides.

3 Arrange a layer of sliced potatoes in the base of the mould or tin, then spoon over about one third of the melted butter, add some truffle slices (if using), and cover with parma ham. Sprinkle with chives and seasoning. Add another layer of potatoes, spoon over more melted butter, then add more truffle slices (if using) and another layer of ham. Sprinkle with chives and seasoning. Add the remaining potatoes, butter, truffle slices and finish with a layer of ham. Fold over the hanging pieces of ham. Cover the whole terrine with clingfilm and press down lightly to firm.

4 Place a flat plate on top of the terrine and weigh down with a large can or something similar. Chill in the refrigerator overnight.

5 Before serving, mix together all the ingredients for the dressing. Demould the terrine by shaking out on to a board. Peel off the clingfilm and cut into 6 even slices. Place each slice on a serving plate and spoon around the dressing. Serve lightly chilled.

This may sound like a dish from a *Star Wars* bistro, but in fact gedi goats' cheese is a fine example of one of the many exciting new English cheeses being made today. I've give it a fusion food twist and served it Mediterranean style with Spanish membrillo quince paste wrapped in parma ham, which has been quickly pan-fried and caramelized. May the force of flavour be with you!

Gedi goats' cheese bruschetta with quince and parma ham

serves 4

150 g (5½ oz) Spanish membrillo or Portuguese marmelo quince paste

4 slices parma ham

4 slices ciabatta bread

olive oil, for brushing and frying

2 good pinches of dried thyme or leaves stripped from 2 fresh sprigs

1 fat garlic clove, halved

300 g (10½ oz) gedi goats' cheese log or another semi-soft chèvre, rinded and sliced

freshly ground black pepper

1 Heat the oven to 200°C (400°F), Gas Mark 6. Meanwhile, cut the quince paste into 4 equal sized slices, then wrap each quince slice in a slice of parma ham. Set aside.

2 Brush the bread with oil and bake in the oven for 10 minutes until lightly crisp and golden brown.

3 Meanwhile, heat a trickle of oil in a frying pan and swirl to coat the surface. Add the ham-wrapped quince and pan-fry for about 2 minutes on each side until just browned, scattering lightly with the thyme.

4 Remove the bread from the oven and quickly rub the surface with the garlic, then top with the cheese. Place a ham and quince slice on top of each bread slice and drizzle over any pan juices. Season and serve immediately.

serving note

This dish is best served with a mixed leaf salad lightly dressed with olive oil and balsamic vinegar.

Figs roasted with blue cheese and proscuitto

When ripe sweet black figs are in season, serve them as a chic hot starter stuffed with nuggets of blue cheese and wrapped in Italian prosciutto. It takes next to no time to prepare and only a few minutes to cook.

serves 4

8 ripe black figs

250 g (9 oz) soft blue cheese, eg roquefort, pipo crème, dolcelatte or blue brie

8 thin slices prosciutto

olive oil, for brushing

2 tbsp balsamic vinegar

2 tbsp chopped fresh mint

freshly ground black pepper

1 Cut the figs almost in half from top to bottom but leaving the halves attached at the base. Open out the 2 halves.

2 Cut the blue cheese into 8 cubes and sandwich between the fig halves. Close up the fig halves.

3 Lay the prosciutto slices flat on a board. Place one stuffed fig on each slice and roll up. Place on a baking sheet and brush lightly with the oil. When nearly ready to serve, heat the oven to 190°C (375°F), Gas Mark 5.

4 Drizzle the vinegar over the figs and bake in the oven for 8–10 minutes until the prosciutto crisps up and before the cheese starts to ooze out of the figs. Serve immediately, with any pan juices spooned over and sprinkled with chopped mint and freshly ground black pepper.

Iberico ham with a herby leaf salad

Dry-cured and smoked, Spanish hams can be served in the same way as parma ham – thinly sliced as a starter or buffet dish. Iberico pigs are fed on wild acorns and live a heavenly porcine existence. Consequently, the flesh tastes divine and the very dark meat is beautifully flavoured and moist.

serves 4

about 250 g (9 oz) Continental-style salad leaves, eg wild rocket, red chard, baby spinach, etc

1 tbsp fresh chervil sprigs

2 tbsp fresh flat leaf parsley leaves

1 tbsp chopped fresh chives

3 tbsp extra virgin olive oil (preferably Spanish)

1 tbsp balsamic or sherry wine vinegar

300 g (10½ oz) thinly sliced iberico ham

freshly ground black pepper

1 Pick over the salad leaves and discard any that are damaged or discoloured. Place in a large bowl and toss with the prepared herbs.

2 Whisk the oil with the vinegar and seasoning. Pour over the salad leaves and herbs and toss well.

3 Pile the salad into a mound in the centre of a large platter. Arrange the slices of ham around it, scrunching it loosely into rosettes if liked. Grind over pepper to taste before serving.

serving note

This succulent dish is best served with slices of country-style bread.

OK – let's talk about speck, baby. These rashers of pig belly grill to a sweet, fragrant crispness. You will find two types in delis – Italian speck, which is quite fatty but flavoursome, and the leaner, smokier Spanish variety. Here, I've teamed it with small cubes of fine British black pudding, which I also adore. Not for me the sticky slabs found on greasy 'caf' plates. I like my black pudding as it should be – a dark, rich burgundy red, with chunky pieces of creamy fat and a full flavour. Chargrilled artichokes in oil – the other star ingredient of this dish – is one of my favourite storecupboard standbys.

Crispy speck, artichoke and black pudding salad

serves 4

125 g (4½ oz) speck, sliced wafer thin

150 g (5½ oz) rocket leaves

a small handful of fresh flat leaf parsley leaves

½ x 200 g (7 oz) jar chargrilled artichokes in oil, drained and sliced

olive oil, for frying

60 g (2¼ oz) top-quality black pudding, cut into 1 cm (½ in) cubes

4 garlic cloves, roughly crushed

½ small red onion, thinly sliced

8 cherry tomatoes, halved or whole

parmesan shavings, to garnish (optional)

dressing

4 tbsp balsamic vinegar

6 tbsp olive oil

sea salt flakes and freshly ground back pepper

1 Heat the grill until hot. Grill the speck rashers until crispy, then drain on kitchen paper. Snip into small pieces with kitchen scissors. Set aside.

2 Whisk the ingredients for the dressing together or place in a screw-top jar and shake to mix. Toss the rocket with the parsley leaves, sliced artichokes and dressing in a large bowl and season well.

3 Heat a frying pan and when you feel a steady heat rising, add a trickle of oil, then toss in the black pudding cubes and the garlic. Fry for about 3 minutes until the black pudding is crisp on all sides.

4 Add the onion and fry for 2 minutes. Add the tomatoes and cook for a further 1–2 minutes. Toss the contents of the pan with the salad and the pieces of speck, check the seasoning and serve immediately. Add a few shavings of parmesan before serving, if liked.

variation

You could use Spanish serrano ham in place of the speck. For an extra twist, bake the serrano ham slices around a wooden rolling pin in a preheated oven, 190°C (375°F), Gas Mark 5, for about 10 minutes until crisp. Leave to cool on kitchen paper, then arrange on top of the salad. You can use these as a flamboyant garnish for other dishes, too.

Bruschetta of smoked beef and melted brie

One of the great joys of owning a deli is that new enterprising food producers bring their wares in for you to try, and I have discovered many great foods as a result. One of these is a hot smoked beef made by one of my local suppliers, Walter Burrough, who in a former life worked as an estate agent, or something of that nature. Smoking all manner of farmed-reared country meats is fast becoming a popular feature of quality British food. This is one of the exciting things I like to do with it – basically serve it on toast! It is equally delicious served with salad and boiled new potatoes.

serves 4

1 whole focaccia loaf

5–6 tbsp olive oil

3–4 tbsp coarse-grain mustard, eg Pommery or Gordons

200 g (7 oz) smoked beef or cold rare cooked beef, thinly sliced

175 g (6 oz) brie de meaux, sliced into wafer-thin wedges

about 200 g (7 oz) mixed salad leaves

2 tbsp roughly chopped fresh parsley

juice of 1 small lemon

sea salt and freshly ground black pepper

1 Heat the grill until hot. Split the focaccia in half widthways, then brush with 2 tbsp of the oil. Toast the cut side under the grill until lightly browned.

2 Spread the toasted side with the mustard and top with the beef slices, then the brie wedges. Brush with 1 tbsp of the oil. Return to the grill until melted and bubbling.

3 Meanwhile, mix the salad leaves with the parsley, then toss with the remaining oil and the lemon juice. Season well and divide between serving plates.

4 Cut each piece of focaccia in half to make 4 portions. Place on top of the salad and serve immediately.

Bresaola is air-cured beef from Italy, served in much the same way as parma ham – that is, wafer thin with one or two simple accompaniments. One of the garnishes I like to serve with it is pieces of lemon zest cooked in sugar syrup. It may sound odd, but it's a winning combination. If you have a swivel vegetable peeler and half an hour to spare, you can make up a batch to store in the refrigerator, ready to serve when you want to impress your dinner guests. Any unused pieces of zest can be stored in the syrup in a jam jar.

Bresaola with confit lemon rind and rocket salad

serves 4

4 unwaxed lemons, washed and dried

85 g (3 oz) caster sugar

300 ml (½ pt) water

200 g (7 oz) wild rocket leaves

3–4 tbsp extra virgin olive oil

200 g (7 oz) bresaola, sliced wafer thin

50 g (1¾ oz) parmesan

sea salt and freshly ground black pepper

1 Peel the zest from the lemons using a swivel vegetable peeler, making sure that you don't include any of the white pith. If long, cut the zest into lengths of about 2 cm (¾ in).

2 Place the sugar and water in a saucepan and heat gently until the sugar is dissolved. Bring to the boil, stirring. Drop in the pieces of zest and simmer for about 15 minutes until they become translucent. Leave to cool in the syrup, then drain well and pat dry with kitchen paper.

3 Season the rocket leaves, then dress with the oil.

4 Lay out the bresaola slices on 4 serving plates, spreading them thinly. Place an equal portion of the rocket salad in the centre of each plate. Sprinkle over as many pieces of zest as you like.

5 Shave the parmesan into wafer-thin slices and scatter over the plates. Grind over pepper and serve.

Main courses

Being a Yorkshire lad, I have to confess that I'm a bit of a 'meat-and-two-veg' man. To me, the main centre of attraction in a meal is a nice chunk of meat or a thick fillet of fish. But I don't just leave the dish at that. Delis are great sources of inspiration and ingredients for adding character to basic dishes and inventing entirely new and exciting ideas.

I've put my favourite deli flavourings and seasonings to creative use in these main courses, whether in marinades and roasts or to add an instant kick to pan-fries. The deli ingredients include olive and herb-flavoured oils; red wine and balsamic vinegars; Asian sauces and pastes; and spices. Olives, capers and nuts all provide contrasts of colour, flavour and texture, while sun-dried and grilled vegetables in oil offer both quality and convenience. Sausages and cured meats make a serious contribution in classic combinations with a twist.

Most of the dishes in this chapter can be served with either creamy mash, perfect fluffy rice or comfortingly sticky fragrant Thai rice, or pasta. But you might also like to try polenta, couscous, or the high-protein South-American grain, quinoa. Sometimes I like to serve a simple accompanying dish of tender-cooked pulses.

Whole sea bass is becoming as popular as salmon for serving at a summer party, although it is quite a bit more expensive. You can find farmed sea bass, flown in from the Mediterranean, but they may be smaller, in which case you will need two. Ask the fishmonger to scale the skin well. You can remove the head and fins, but the fish looks more majestic intact. Roasting the limes alongside makes them more juicy and fragrant.

Sea bass with summer herbs and roasted limes

serves 4–6

1 whole sea bass, about 1.3–1.8 kg (3–4 lb), scaled and gutted

100 ml (3½ fl oz) olive oil

3 large limes

3 tbsp chopped fresh mixed herbs, eg marjoram, parsley, basil, dill or oregano, plus a few whole sprigs to garnish (optional)

sea salt and freshly ground black pepper

1 Wash the fish thoroughly under cold running water, especially the body cavity, paying attention to rubbing out any clotted blood along the backbone. Pat dry with kitchen paper. Make slashes diagonally across the fish, about 4–6 in all, on both sides. Place the fish in a roasting pan and brush lightly with some of the oil.

2 Grate the zest of 1 lime and squeeze the juice. Mix with the chopped herbs and press the mixture into the slashes. Don't worry if it looks rather messy.

3 Heat the oven to 200°C (400°F), Gas Mark 6. Cut the other 2 limes in half and nestle alongside the fish. Season everything well and drizzle over the remaining oil.

4 Roast the fish in the oven, uncovered, for about 25–30 minutes until the flesh feels just firm when pressed. If you want to double-check that it is cooked, part some of the flesh down the backbone to see if it flakes.

5 Squeeze the juice from the roasted limes over the fish and serve on a platter with the pan juices trickled over. It is quite chic to use the squeezed lime shells as a garnish, along with some sprigs of the herbs you used, if liked.

A whole sea bass is a wonderful treat and really comes into its own when simply roasted with a handful of pinenuts, lots of garlic and lemon. And the pan juices provide the perfect sauce.

Sea bass with pinenuts, artichokes and tomatoes

serves 4

1 whole sea bass, about 1 kg (2 lb 4 oz), scaled and gutted

olive oil, for roasting

40 g (1½ oz) pinenuts

2 lemons, 1 thinly sliced, 1 squeezed for juice

6 ripe plum tomatoes, halved lengthways

6–10 garlic cloves (to taste), unpeeled

3 shallots, chopped

2 sprigs of fresh thyme

200 g (7 oz) jar chargrilled artichokes in oil, drained and patted dry

2 tbsp chopped fresh parsley

about 100 g (3½ oz) rocket leaves

sea salt and freshly ground black pepper

1 Make sure the bass is thoroughly clean inside by washing under cold running water. Pat dry with kitchen paper. Heat the oven to 190°C (375°F), Gas Mark 5.

2 Rub the skin of the sea bass with a little olive oil and place in a roasting pan. Season well. Sprinkle over the pinenuts and lemon juice. Roast in the oven, uncovered, for about 20–25 minutes until the flesh feels quite firm and bouncy when pressed with the back of a fork. This indicates that it is almost cooked.

3 Meanwhile, place the tomatoes, cut side up, in a separate roasting pan. Trickle over a little olive oil, season well, then scatter over the garlic cloves, shallots and sprigs of thyme. Roast for 15 minutes until softened. Set aside to cool a little.

4 Slice and season the artichokes, then toss gently with the slightly cooled tomatoes.

5 Remove the fish from the oven and leave for 15 minutes before serving. Scoop off the pinenuts and gently mix with the tomatoes and artichokes. Cut the fish into fillets by inserting a sharp pointed knife into the backbone and loosening the flesh. Lift it from the bones, then pull away the whole skeleton from the tail to the head to reveal the underside fillet. Cut both fillets in half.

6 Squeeze the roasted garlic cloves from their skins and roughly chop. Add to the tomatoes and artichokes with the parsley and rocket leaves. Toss gently to mix.

7 Divide the salad between serving plates and place the fish on top. Season well, drizzle over any pan juices and serve.

Sea bass with sprouting wheatgerm salad

Sprouting wheatgerm is a fantastic ingredient and is available in health food shops and some delicatessens; although if unavailable, crushed tinned chick peas make a good alternative. In this recipe the wheatgerm works well with Mediterranean vegetables as a salad and it's the perfect accompaniment to the sea bass.

serves 2

125 g (4½ oz) sprouting wheatgerm

2 plum tomatoes, halved lengthways and seeded

1 shallot, chopped finely

1 fat garlic clove, chopped

1 tbsp black olives, pitted and chopped

2 pimientos (red peppers) in oil, well drained and chopped

1 tbsp chopped fresh basil

2 tbsp extra virgin olive oil

1 tbsp balsamic vinegar

2 sea bass fillets, about 175 g (6 oz) each, skin on and neatly trimmed

4 chargrilled artichokes in oil from a jar, well drained

1 tbsp chopped fresh parsley

juice of 1 lemon

sea salt and freshly ground black pepper

1 Place the wheatgerm in a pan, cover with cold water and bring to the boil. Reduce the heat and simmer gently, uncovered, for 45 minutes. Drain and set aside.

2 Cut the tomato halves into thin strips, then cut these into fine dice. Mix with the shallot, garlic, olives, pimientos and basil. Season well and toss with 1 tbsp of the oil and the vinegar. Set aside.

3 Heat a heavy-based non-stick frying pan. Rub the bass skin with the remaining oil. When you feel a good heat rising from the pan, add the bass, skin side down, and cook for about 5 minutes until almost cooked. Turn over carefully to cook the other side. Season, remove from the pan and keep warm.

4 Thinly slice the artichokes, add to the pan and heat through for about 2 minutes. Transfer to 2 warmed serving plates.

5 Mix the cooked wheatgerm with the parsley, lemon juice and seasoning and spoon on top of the artichokes. Spoon the tomato and pimiento mixture around the edge and finally place a cooked sea bass fillet on the top. Serve immediately.

Monkfish is a strange creature – a white fish with the smooth texture of shellfish. It slices conveniently into neat nuggets, and blends well with punchy flavours such as cracked black pepper, mustard and dill. Monkfish tails are sold ready-skinned, but ask the fishmonger to remove the long cartilaginous bone for you. Cut off as much of the grey membrane as you can before cutting into medallions – a razor-sharp filleting knife will make the task easier.

Pepper-crusted monkfish with mustard dill sauce

serves 4

1 monkfish tail, about 500 g (1 lb 2 oz), filleted and skinned

2 tbsp olive oil, for frying

about 3 tbsp cracked black pepper (*see* step 2 of salad on page 18)

sea salt and freshly ground black pepper

sauce

1 tbsp olive oil

1 shallot, chopped

1 garlic clove, chopped

3 tbsp white wine

100 ml (3½ fl oz) double cream

3 tbsp coarse-grain mustard, eg Pommery or Gordons

2 tbsp chopped fresh dill

1 Trim the monkfish (*see* recipe introduction), then cut into medallions about 2.5 cm (1 in) thick. Season with a little salt and press each medallion lightly into the cracked pepper to coat. Place in the refrigerator.

2 To make the sauce, heat the oil in a frying pan, add the shallot and garlic and sauté for 3 minutes. Add the wine and cook until evaporated. Stir in the cream and bring to the boil, then add the mustard, dill and seasoning. Reduce the heat and keep warm.

3 Wipe out the pan with kitchen paper. Heat the oil for frying until very hot, add the monkfish medallions and cook for about 2 minutes on each side until browned and just firm when pressed. Remove and drain on kitchen paper.

4 Place the medallions on 4 warmed serving plates and spoon the sauce around.

serving note

Serve with the Bubble and squeak cakes, page 82, and a salad of crisp mixed leaves.

Seared tuna with quinoa and kalamata olives

Much was made a few years ago of a new supergrain called quinoa (pronounced 'keenwa'), said to be an ancient food of the Incas. Higher in protein than other grains, it also happens to taste good when tossed with ingredients such as lime, olives, garlic and chilli. I like to serve it with a juicy cooked tuna steak, but other seafood or pan-fried chicken would be equally fine.

serves 4

200 g (7 oz) quinoa

500 ml (18 fl oz) water

grated zest and juice of 1 lime

1 large fresh red chilli, deseeded and chopped

1 garlic clove, crushed

3 tbsp kalamata olives, pitted and chopped

2 tbsp deseeded and chopped cucumber

4 tbsp chopped fresh mixed herbs, eg parsley, dill or chervil

4 tbsp olive oil

1 plum tomato, deseeded and finely chopped

3 tbsp red wine vinegar

4 tuna steaks, about 125 g (4½ oz) each

sea salt and freshly ground black pepper

1 Rinse the quinoa well in cold running water to remove any bitterness. Drain well. Place in a saucepan with the water. Bring to the boil, then reduce the heat, cover and simmer for about 15 minutes until the grains are tender and translucent. Drain to remove any remaining liquid and return to the pan. Stir in the lime zest and juice, chilli, garlic, olives, cucumber, half the herbs and 1 tbsp of the oil. Season well and set aside.

2 Mix the remaining herbs with the chopped tomato, 2 tbsp of the oil, vinegar and seasoning for the dressing. Set aside.

3 Rub the remaining oil over the tuna steaks and season. Heat a ridged griddle pan or heavy-based frying pan until you feel a good heat rising. Add the tuna steaks and cook for about 2 minutes on each side if you like your tuna pink in the middle, or for a few minutes longer for medium cooked steaks.

4 Reheat the quinoa and divide between warmed serving plates. Top with the tuna steaks and spoon the dressing either over the top of the steak or around the edge before serving.

ingredients note

Purple kalamata olives from Greece are regarded by some gourmets as probably the best in the world. They are certainly amongst the largest!

This is another of my best-loved fish and sausage combinations – the majestic turbot, a meaty flat fish, and the French boudin sausage. You can use black or white boudin, which is available from many good delis. British black pudding, however, is softer and crumbles, so is not a good substitute. Soulful black-eye beans peas give this dish an American twist.

Turbot with boudin and black-eye beans

serves 4

200g (7oz) black-eye beans, soaked overnight and drained

1 onion, chopped

2 fat garlic cloves, crushed

1 carrot, chopped

1 medium leek, chopped

2 tbsp olive oil, plus extra, for brushing

250g (9oz) boudin sausage, blanc or noir, diced

450ml (16 floz) fresh chicken stock (buy ready-made in a tub)

1 sprig of fresh thyme

4 turbot, halibut or swordfish fillets, about 150g (5½oz) each, skinned

3 tbsp Forvm red wine vinegar (*see* ingredients note)

a good knob of butter

2 tbsp chopped fresh parsley

2 tbsp basil oil

sea salt and freshly ground black pepper

1 Place the beans in a saucepan, cover with cold water and bring to the boil. Cook on a medium boil for 10 minutes. Drain and set aside. Heat the oven to 180°C (350°F), Gas Mark 4.

2 Place the onion, garlic, carrot, leek and the 2 tbsp olive oil in a cast-iron saucepan or casserole or flameproof casserole and heat until the contents start to sizzle. Sauté for about 5 minutes, then add the diced sausage and cook for about 3 minutes.

3 Add the stock and the beans. Bring to the boil and add the sprig of thyme and seasoning. Cover and transfer the pot to the oven. Cook for about 45 minutes until the beans are tender.

4 Brush the fish fillets with a little olive oil and season. Place in an ovenproof dish and bake, uncovered, for 10–12 minutes until the fish is just firm to the touch but not overcooked. Remove and keep warm.

5 Place the bean pot back on the stove, add the vinegar and cook, uncovered, for about 10 minutes until the liquid is reduced by a third. Remove the beans and vegetables from the broth with a slotted spoon and place on warmed serving plates.

6 Whisk the butter into the broth until it turns glossy, then stir in the parsley. Spoon the sauce over the beans and place the turbot on top. Drizzle around the basil oil.

ingredients note

I rate Spanish Forvm wine vinegar, used here to spike the bean broth, as possibly the best wine vinegar available. It is made from Cabernet Sauvignon wine, and is so mellow that you can almost drink it neat.

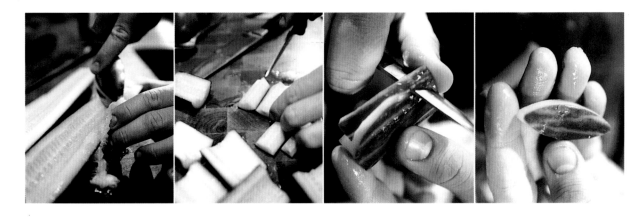

5 tbsp olive oil, plus extra,
for brushing

4 red onions, thinly sliced

2 fat garlic cloves,
crushed

4 tbsp red wine

5 tbsp balsamic vinegar

1 sprig of fresh thyme

2 tbsp caster sugar

2 tbsp chopped
fresh parsley

½ cucumber

4 salmon fillets, about
150g (5½oz) each,
skin on

2 ripe tomatoes,
halved, deseeded and
finely chopped

4 tbsp fig balsamic vinegar

sprigs of fresh chervil,
to garnish

sea salt and freshly
ground black pepper

Chargrilled salmon is always well received, and it is one of the most versatile fish, suiting a wide assortment of flavours. Here, I match it with a rich red onion relish swirled with a really unusual vinegar – fig balsamic, a syrupy liquid made by steeping figs in a Californian balsamic wine vinegar. Don't expect a thin liquid; it has the consistency of a coulis. Other flavours in this range of extraordinary vinegars include blackcurrant and cherry. The whole dish has a taste of Scarborough Beach meets the Italian Riviera!

Salmon with red onion pickle

1 To make the 'pickle', heat 4 tbsp of the oil in a saucepan, add the onions and garlic and sauté gently for about 5 minutes. Add the wine, vinegar, thyme and sugar.

2 Bring to the boil, then reduce the heat, cover and gently simmer for about 20 minutes. Uncover and continue cooking, stirring occasionally, until the liquid has evaporated away and the onions are meltingly soft. Stir in the parsley, set aside and leave to cool.

3 Meanwhile, halve the cucumber lengthways and scoop out the seeds. Cut the flesh into 4cm (1½in) batons. (If you have a chef's turning knife, you might like to try your hand at 'turning' them into barrel shapes.) Heat the remaining 1 tbsp oil in a small saucepan, add the cucumber and sauté gently for about 5 minutes until hot and just soft. Season and set aside.

4 Season the salmon. Brush a heavy-based ridged griddle pan with a light film of oil. Heat until very hot, add the salmon steaks, skin side down, and cook for about 4 minutes. Turn over carefully and cook the other side for about 2–3 minutes.

5 Spoon some of the relish in the centre of warmed dinner plates, slide a salmon fillet on top, skin side up, and scatter around the cucumber batons and chopped tomatoes. Drizzle 1 tbsp fig balsamic vinegar per serving around the cucumber and tomatoes and over the salmon. Garnish with the chervil sprigs and serve.

serving note

New potatoes are the best accompaniment.

Salmon with wild garlic sauce and champ

Champ is simply creamy mashed potatoes with the addition of chopped spring onions. To make it extra special, I serve it with a nicely cooked fish fillet and a quick sauce of wilted wild garlic. I appreciate that wild garlic is not readily on sale except in a few highly specialized country greengrocers. But in many parts of the country it grows in abundance along shady lanes and in woodlands in early summer. You cannot fail to notice it – the pungency wafts towards you well before you spot the lush green leaves and small white flowers. Out of season, use shredded young spinach leaves.

serves 4

500 g (1 lb 2 oz) large new potatoes, scrubbed to remove skin

100 ml (3½ fl oz) milk

40 g (1½ oz) butter

4–6 spring onions, chopped

1 tbsp olive oil

4 salmon fillets, about 125 g (4½ oz) each, skinned

5 tbsp Noilly Prat

200 ml (7 fl oz) single cream

2 garlic cloves, crushed

a small handful of wild garlic leaves or baby spinach leaves, roughly shredded

sea salt and freshly ground black pepper

1 Boil the potatoes in a saucepan of lightly salted water for about 12 minutes until just tender. Drain well and return to the pan to dry off a little over the lingering heat.

2 Meanwhile, place the milk in a saucepan and heat until on the point of boiling. Heat half the butter in a frying pan, add the spring onions and sauté for 1–2 minutes. Using a fork, mash the potatoes, gradually working in the hot milk, until you have a smooth paste. You may not need all the milk – it depends on the variety of potato. Beat the spring onions into the potato, season well and keep warm.

3 Heat the remaining butter with the oil in a large frying pan. Season the fish, add to the pan and fry for about 2 minutes on each side, or longer for thicker-cut fillets, until just firm.

4 Remove the salmon from the pan and keep warm. Add the Noilly Prat and allow to bubble for 1–2 minutes, then add the cream and crushed garlic and cook for about 2 minutes until reduced by about a third.

5 Season the sauce, then add the shredded wild garlic leaves or spinach and cook for a few seconds until wilted.

6 To serve, spoon the champ on to the centre of warmed serving plates. Place a fish fillet on top and spoon over the wild garlic sauce.

serving note

I like to garnish this dish with some deep-fried enoki mushrooms – long, spindly fungi that grow in clumps. They are sometimes available from larger supermarkets.

There are some delicious Asian sauces that add instant flavour to quick marinades and pan-fries. I quickly made up this recipe on a television set with Ken Hom, the well-known Chinese chef, in my keenness to show him that a Yorkshireman could cook Chinese. The marinade has since served me well on various occasions, adding a great depth of flavour for very little effort. Brill is a meaty flat fish that is increasingly available from fishmongers. If you cannot find it, sole is a good substitute. You'll need to buy fresh pork belly rashers or a whole piece of pork belly and marinate it the night before.

serves 4

500 g (1 lb 2 oz) pork belly, in one piece, or thick-cut rashers, rinded

4 brill or sole fillets, about 150 g (5½ oz) each

melted butter, for brushing

about 400 g (14 oz) pak or bok choy (Chinese greens)

sunflower oil, for stir-frying

a few drops of sesame oil

sea salt and freshly ground black pepper

marinade

2 tbsp tomato purée

½ plump fresh red chilli, deseeded and chopped

1 tsp Chinese five spice powder

1 fat garlic clove, crushed

1 tbsp grated fresh root ginger or ginger purée

1 tbsp Thai fish sauce

1 tbsp dark soy sauce (preferably Tamari)

1 tbsp sake or very dry sherry

1 tbsp demerara sugar

Brill with Chinese lardons and green leaves

1 Place the pork belly or rashers in a food bag. Blend the ingredients for the marinade in a food processor or blender to form a paste, or mix by hand, and pour into the bag. Rub well into the meat, then seal the bag, place in the refrigerator and leave to marinate overnight.

2 Heat the oven to 180°C (350°F), Gas Mark 4. Tip the pork and marinade into a roasting pan and cook, uncovered, for 30–40 minutes until the meat is tender and the top nicely browned. Leave to cool, then cut the meat into small cubes.

3 Season and brush the brill or sole with a little melted butter. Heat the grill until hot. Grill the fish for about 5–8 minutes without turning, otherwise the flesh may break up. Set aside.

4 Chop the greens into big pieces. Heat the sunflower oil in a wok, add the pork cubes and stir-fry for 1–2 minutes until hot. Add the chopped greens and stir-fry quickly until wilted. Drizzle over a few drops of sesame oil to flavour and divide between warmed serving plates. Place a brill fillet on top of each mound of greens and serve immediately.

Halibut parcels with capers and Pernod

In wine-growing regions of the world, food is often wrapped in vine leaves and cooked in the embers of a wood fire or barbecue, especially fish which takes just minutes to cook. You can replicate this method of cooking using greaseproof paper. Firm meaty fish, such as halibut, salmon or monkfish, are the most suitable. Capers and the aniseed-flavoured Pernod are classic accompanying flavourings.

serves 4

4 halibut steaks, about 200g (7oz) each

4 tbsp capers in brine, drained

4 tbsp Pernod

50g (1¾oz) butter, cut into 4 cubes

juice of 1 lemon

4 slices lemon

sea salt and freshly ground black pepper

1 Heat the oven to 190°C (375°F), Gas Mark 5. Cut 4 x 25cm (10 in) squares of greaseproof paper. Lay them flat and place a halibut steak in the centre of each. Season, then scatter each steak with 1 tbsp of capers and 1 tbsp Pernod. Add a cube of butter, sprinkle over lemon juice and top with a lemon slice.

2 Fold over or scrunch up the paper to form parcels and place in a baking dish. Bake the parcels in the oven for 15–20 minutes until just firm to the touch (feel through the paper).

3 Leave the parcels to stand for 5 minutes then transfer each parcel to a warmed serving plate and spoon the capers on the top.

serving note

Serve this dish with mashed potato, baby new potatoes or rice and a bowl of lightly cooked whole green beans.

Halibut steaks with beansprout and coriander salad

serves 4

200 g (7 oz) fresh
beansprouts

2 tbsp roughly chopped
fresh coriander leaves

1 shallot, finely chopped

grated zest and juice
of 1 lemon

1 fat fresh red chilli,
deseeded and thinly sliced

1–2 tbsp olive oil

2 halibut steaks, about
200 g (7 oz) each

Plum chutney
(*see* page 134)

sea salt and freshly
ground black pepper

Halibut is a large flat fish caught in the cold, dark waters of the North Atlantic, which gives it a fine flavour and firm texture. Sold in meaty steaks, sometimes with a small central bone, I find it suits flash pan-frying very well and teams up nicely with my Plum chutney, page 134, and this easy salad. This is real fusion food.

1 Wash the beansprouts in a colander and shake dry. Tip into a bowl and add the chopped coriander, shallot, lemon zest and juice, chilli and seasoning. Mix well and set aside.

2 When ready to serve, heat a heavy-based frying pan until you feel a good heat rising. Add the oil, then the halibut, skin side down, and fry for 5 minutes until crispy. Carefully flip over and cook the other side for about 2 minutes until the flesh feels firm when pressed.

3 Divide the salad between serving plates and place a fish fillet on top. Spoon a little chutney on to each plate and serve.

This is New British food with a twist. We are great cod lovers in this country, but sadly, as stocks dwindle, so do the size and quality of the fish on sale. We love thick, meaty middle-cut fillets of cod, but more often than not we now get thinner pieces from younger fish. They still taste great, but just be prepared to pay a high price for them. Coastal regions of the UK still keep the tradition of selling small pots of tasty little pinky-brown shrimps set in a little butter, known as potted shrimps. To make them even more 'shrimpy', I like to add a few chopped cold water prawns. Sometimes sold as North Atlantic prawns, these have a full, sweet-salty taste of the wild ocean. Seafood from icy-cold waters tastes much nicer than its tropical water cousins.

Pan-fried cod with vanilla shrimp butter

serves 4

2 small tubs potted shrimps, about 50 g (1¾ oz) each, at room temperature

100 g (3½ oz) unsalted butter, softened

100 g (3½ oz) peeled cold cooked water prawns, thawed if frozen and patted dry

2 tbsp chopped fresh parsley

1 vanilla pod

3 tbsp extra virgin olive oil

4 fresh cod fillets, about 150–200 g (5½–7 oz) each

1 tbsp balsamic vinegar

100 g (3½ oz) mixed salad leaves

sea salt and freshly ground black pepper

1 Mix the potted shrimps with the unsalted butter in a bowl. Chop the prawns quite finely and add to the shrimp mixture with the parsley and plenty of pepper. Mix well.

2 Slit the vanilla pod lengthways and scrape out the seeds with the tip of a knife. Add the seeds to the shrimp butter. (Re-use the pod for making vanilla sugar – *see* ingredients note, page 119.) Shape the shrimp butter into a log on a sheet of clingfilm and roll neatly until smooth on the outside. Chill in the refrigerator for about 30 minutes until firm.

3 When ready to serve, heat 1 tbsp of the oil in a large frying pan. Season the cod and fry, skin side down, on a medium heat for about 5–7 minutes until the flesh is about

three-quarters cooked (you can check this simply by pressing the flesh; it should feel just a little springy). Turn the fish over carefully to cook the other side, but turn off the heat so that it cooks gently.

4 Cut the butter into neat discs, allowing about 2 per serving. Add any end pieces of butter to the pan to flavour the cod.

5 Mix the remaining oil with the vinegar and seasoning. Place the salad leaves in a bowl, add the dressing and toss well.

6 Divide the salad between serving plates. Arrange the cod fillets on the dressed leaves, with the discs of shrimp butter on top. Grind over some black pepper and serve immediately.

Cheat's coq au vin

serves 4

8 cooked joints of chicken,
on the bone – a mixture of
breasts and thighs or legs

25 g (1 oz) butter

1 tbsp olive oil

4 garlic cloves, chopped

2 red onions, sliced

150 g (5½ oz) pancetta,
in one piece, rinded
and chopped

250 g (9 oz) button
mushrooms

a good pinch of
dried thyme

300 ml (½ pt) red wine

500 ml (18 fl oz) fresh
chicken stock (buy
ready-made in a tub)

150 ml (¼ pt) double
cream

2 tbsp chopped
fresh parsley

sea salt and freshly
ground black pepper

One evening I invited a new girlfriend to supper, intending to wow her with the classic French dish, *coq au vin*. Typically, I was late back from work. Undaunted and unabashed, I picked up a bargain bucket of fried chicken from the local takeaway and spent the 15 minutes before she arrived stripping the chicken of its crispy coating and making a simple red wine sauce. The meal was a great success, so either she didn't notice or was just too polite to say anything!

1 Skin the cooked chicken pieces and set aside.

2 Heat the butter with the oil in a large cast-iron or flameproof casserole, add the garlic, onions and pancetta and sauté for about 5 minutes until softened. Add the mushrooms and thyme and sauté for 5 minutes.

3 Pour in the wine, bring to the boil and continue boiling, uncovered, for about 5 minutes until the sauce is reduced by half. Pour in the stock and bring back to the boil.

4 Season and add the chicken to the sauce. Reduce the heat and simmer for a good 5 minutes until the chicken is thoroughly heated through. Remove the chicken pieces to a warmed serving dish with a slotted spoon.

5 Increase the heat and boil the sauce until reduced by about half. Reduce the heat, stir in the cream and gently heat through.

6 Pour the sauce over the chicken pieces, sprinkle with parsley. Serve.

serving note

Creamy mash or rice goes particularly well with this dish.

Pan-fried chicken with chilli beans, fennel and pancetta

This is a great meal for the end of a hard-working day. Buy the ingredients on your way home from work and within half an hour you'll have a great tasting dish full of punchy flavours. All it needs is a loaf of crusty bread and a simple green salad – oh, and a glass or two of crisp white wine.

serves 4

2 tbsp extra virgin olive oil, plus extra, for drizzling

4 skinless, boneless chicken breasts, about 150 g (5½ oz) each

2 shallots, chopped

4 garlic cloves, chopped

1 large fresh red chilli, deseeded and chopped

1 small bulb of fennel, thinly sliced

400 g (14 oz) can flageolet beans, rinsed and drained

grated zest and juice of 1 lemon

3 tbsp chopped mixed fresh herbs, eg parsley, mint or basil

8 thin slices of pancetta

sea salt and freshly ground black pepper

1 Heat a large heavy-based non-stick frying pan until you feel a good heat rising. Add about 1 tbsp of the oil, then add the chicken breasts and pan-fry for about 5 minutes on each side until firm when pressed with the back of a fork. Season well and set aside in the pan. They will keep warm without extra heating.

2 Heat the remaining 1 tbsp oil in a separate pan, add the shallots, garlic, chilli and fennel and stir-fry for about 5 minutes until softened.

3 Add the beans and seasoning to taste, then heat through until piping hot. Stir in the lemon zest and juice and fresh herbs.

4 Meanwhile, heat the grill until hot. Grill the pancetta until crisp, then drain on kitchen paper.

5 Divide the bean and fennel mixture between 4 warmed serving plates. Slice the chicken breasts into medallions and arrange on top, then add 2 slices of pancetta to each plate, which you can either crumble or leave whole. Drizzle over any chicken pan juices and a little extra oil.

This is a quick and impressive dinner party dish. You'll need to track down a spicy fennel and pinenut pâté called pâté di finocchietto from – yes, you've guessed it – a good deli. All the other ingredients are readily available. For the duck breasts, use either Lincolnshire duck or the darker French Barbary breasts which are larger. Serve with pasta or creamy mash.

Duck breasts with fennel pâté and apples

serves 2

1 medium-sized bulb of fennel, sliced thinly, fronds reserved, for garnishing

1 golden delicious apple, cored and cut into 8 wedges

1 fat garlic clove, crushed

1 shallot, chopped

2 tbsp olive oil

a knob of butter

1 tbsp runny honey

2 fresh duck breasts, about 150–200 g (5½–7 oz) each

90 g (3¼ oz) jar pâté di finocchietto

2 tbsp toasted pinenuts

sea salt and freshly ground black pepper

1 Place the fennel, apple, garlic and shallot in a saucepan with the oil and butter. Heat until it starts to sizzle, then sauté gently for about 10 minutes, stirring carefully until softened. Turn up the heat towards the end of the cooking time to colour the apple wedges. Season and keep warm

2 Heat the honey in a non-stick frying pan. Slash the fat side of the duck breasts 3–4 times, add to the pan and fry, skin side down, for about 5 minutes until the skin becomes a glossy dark brown. Be careful not to let the fat begin to smoke. If it does, pour it away.

3 Turn the breasts and cook on the other side for 5 minutes. The breasts are nicest served slightly pink inside, which you can check by pressing them with the back of a fork. They should feel lightly springy but not too bouncy. If you prefer them less pink, then cook for a few minutes longer, but don't overcook.

4 Season the duck in the pan, then remove and leave to stand for 5 minutes. Meanwhile, reheat the fennel and apple mixture.

5 Slice the breasts diagonally into medallions. Spoon the fennel and apple mixture on to the centre of warmed serving plates. Arrange the duck pieces on top. Beat the pâté until runny, then trickle over the duck. Scatter over the pinenuts and garnish with the fennel fronds. (In a restaurant, I would deep-fry the fennel fronds, but you may well think this is not worth the effort.)

Honeyed duck confit with crispy seaweed and creamy mash

serves 2

2 duck legs, confited in their own fat, homemade or from a can or jar

4 tbsp clear honey

3 tbsp olive oil

leaves stripped from 2–3 sprigs of fresh thyme

300 g (10½ oz) mashing potatoes, eg maris piper, king edward or desirée, peeled and chopped

3 tbsp hot milk

a small knob of butter

100 ml (3½ fl oz) red wine

250 ml (9 fl oz) fresh chicken stock (buy ready-made in a tub)

55 g (2 oz) crispy seaweed

sea salt and freshly ground black pepper

You can buy, or prepare yourself, plump, tender duck legs that have been cooked deliciously slowly in their own fat. Known as duck confit, they are ideal for many dishes.

1 Heat the oven to 180°C (350°F), Gas Mark 4. Scrape the fat from the duck legs and place in a roasting pan. (Don't waste the fat – it's wonderful for frying eggs or roasting potatoes.)

2 Whisk the honey and oil together and smear over the duck legs. Sprinkle over the thyme leaves. Roast the legs in the oven for about 20 minutes, spooning the honey glaze over the legs 2–3 times.

3 Meanwhile, boil the potatoes in a saucepan of lightly salted water for about 15 minutes until just tender. Drain, then mash with a fork, gradually beating in the hot milk, butter and plenty of seasoning.

4 Place the wine and stock in a saucepan, bring to the boil and continue boiling until reduced by two-thirds. Season well.

5 Spoon the mashed potato on to the centre of warmed serving plates, sprinkle the seaweed round the mash and sit the duck legs on top. Scrape any meaty bits from the roasting pan and sprinkle over, then pour over the reduced red wine sauce and serve immediately.

ingredients note

To make duck confit, take two duck legs and weigh them. Measure 15 g (½ oz) of salt per 1 kg (2 lb 4 oz) of meat and sprinkle the salt with fresh thyme over the duck legs. Store in the fridge for at least 12 hours. Melt duck fat (available in tins from delis) in a pan over a low heat and bring to a simmer. Place the chilled duck legs in the fat and cook very gently for 1½–2 hours, do not boil. Take off the heat and leave to cool in the fat.

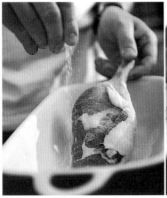  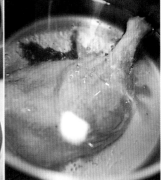

Loins of lamb with cumin and almond-dressed artichokes

serves 4

4 whole loin lamb fillets, about 200 g (7 oz) each

4 tbsp whole cumin seeds

600 g (1 lb 5 oz) Jerusalem artichokes, peeled (use a swivel peeler)

60 g (2¼ oz) butter

2 tbsp olive oil

6 tbsp redcurrant balsamic vinegar (or good-quality, aged balsamic vinegar)

½ small red pepper, cored, deseeded and finely chopped

2 tbsp chopped fresh chervil or parsley

2 tbsp almond oil

sea salt and freshly ground black pepper

Jerusalem artichokes are one of the winter vegetables I greatly enjoy using in cooking, despite their knobbly skins. The name, incidentally, has nothing to do with the Holy City, but is derived from the Italian word for sunflower – girasole – which the plant resembles. In this recipe, I pan-fry them in butter and oil, and use a fruity redcurrant balsamic vinegar from California, sweet almond oil and cumin for flavouring. Loins of lamb (also known as cannons) are the long, narrow, round pieces of meat found in the saddle of a lamb.

1 Trim the loins of all fat so that they are neatly round in shape. Lightly crush the cumin seeds using a pestle and mortar, or use an electric grinder but take care not to grind them too finely. Reserve 1 tbsp of the cumin seeds for later use.

2 Sprinkle the ground cumin on a sheet of foil or paper and roll the loins in the spice to coat. Set aside.

3 Slice the artichokes thinly (drop them immediately into lemony water if preparing ahead to prevent discoloration, since they quickly turn brown once cut). Heat about three-quarters of the butter with 1 tbsp of the olive oil in a frying pan. Add the sliced artichokes and pan-fry for about 10 minutes, stirring occasionally, until tender. Add seasoning, then stir in the vinegar, the reserved cumin seeds, the pepper, half the chervil or parsley and the almond oil. Simmer for about a further 5 minutes. Keep warm.

4 Meanwhile, heat the oven to 200°C (400°F), Gas Mark 6. Heat the remaining olive oil and butter in a heavy-based frying pan, add the loins and cook until evenly browned all over. Transfer to a roasting pan and cook in the oven for about 12 minutes until slightly springy when pressed with the back of a fork. This indicates that they are medium rare. If you like well-done lamb, cook for a few minutes longer. Let the lamb stand for 5 minutes, then slice into medallions.

5 Spoon the artichokes on to the centre of warmed serving plates. Arrange the lamb on top and sprinkle over the remaining chervil or parsley. Trickle over any pan juices and serve.

variation

If you can't buy artichokes, you could substitute baby parsnips.

A simple, full-flavoured, no-nonsense way of cooking a nice leg (or rolled shoulder) of lamb. It's really an adaptation of a recipe I cooked frequently at Anthony Worrall Thompson's 190 Queen's Gate restaurant in South Kensington, London, where we would braise lamb shanks for 24 hours until they were meltingly tender. Boy, were they popular! We would get through hundreds of shanks each week. These days, you have to pay a premium price for them.

Anchovy and garlic-studded roast lamb

serves 4

1 boned and rolled leg or shoulder of lamb, about 2.5–3 kg (5½ lb–6½ lb)

50 g (1¾ oz) can anchovies in oil, drained

7–8 fat garlic cloves, halved lengthways

about 15 sprigs fresh rosemary

olive oil (optional)

sea salt and freshly ground black pepper

1 Heat the oven to 180°C (350°F), Gas Mark 4. Stab the lamb about 15 times or so with a sharp pointed knife.

2 Pat the drained anchovies dry with kitchen paper and cut in half widthways. Roll each piece of anchovy around a halved garlic clove and a rosemary sprig, then push into the stab holes. You may need to make more holes.

3 If the lamb is very lean on top, brush over a little oil to moisten. Season the lamb and place in a roasting pan and roast in the oven for 1–1¼ hours until the meat is very tender. When the lamb is cooked, let it rest for about 15 minutes before carving.

serving note

Serve the lamb in thickly carved slices with the Celeriac remoulade, page 72.

Roast pork with balsamic butter bean broth

serves 6

1 pork joint (loin, lean-rolled belly or boneless rolled shoulder) about 1.3 kg (3 lb), rinded

2 tbsp Dijon mustard

2 tbsp clear honey

500 ml (18 fl oz) fresh chicken stock (buy ready-made in a tub)

2 tbsp balsamic vinegar

400 g (14 oz) can butter beans, rinsed and drained

a good knob of butter

2 tbsp coarse-grain mustard, eg Pommery or Gordons (optional)

2–3 tbsp chopped mixed fresh herbs, eg parsley, dill, oregano and basil

sea salt or freshly ground black pepper

Pork and beans are natural partners. They can be chic and sophisticated or homely and satisfying. This is an adaptation of a dish I make using a trio of pork cuts – lean loin, fillet and a good chunk of fattier belly. But you can use just one of these cuts, or opt for a rolled shoulder of pork that combines lean and fat in one joint. The apple and potato mash (*see* serving note) with the balsamic-flavoured butter beans make this a truly memorable dish.

1 Heat the oven to 180°C (350°F), Gas Mark 4. Spread the Dijon mustard, and then the honey over the pork and season well. Roast the joint in the oven for about 1 hour 45 minutes until tender.

2 Meanwhile, place the stock and vinegar in a saucepan, bring to the boil and continue boiling until reduced by a half. Add the beans and cook for about 5 minutes. Season, stir in a knob of butter and set aside.

3 When the pork is cooked, spread the top with the coarse-grain mustard, if using, and press on the chopped fresh herbs. Let the joint stand for 10 minutes to firm up a little before carving into neat slices. Meanwhile, reheat the beans and serve with the sliced pork.

serving note

Serve this dish with a simple but effective apple and potato mash – grated apple beaten into standard mashed potato. For best results use good mashing potatoes, eg maris piper, king edward or desirée, and golden delicious or granny smith apples.

Calves' liver with port-flavoured pan juices

You can cook this dish in just five minutes flat using a good-quality, ready-made fresh pasta or a decent dried variety, tossed with some fresh or dried sage.

serves 2

25 g (1 oz) butter

1 tbsp olive oil

250 g (9 oz) calves' liver, thinly sliced and cut in half lengthways

about 4 tbsp port or Madeira

2 tsp red wine vinegar

100 ml (3½ fl oz) fresh beef or chicken stock (buy ready-made in a tub)

250 g (9 oz) fresh or 200 g (7 oz) dried ribbon pasta

½ tbsp chopped fresh sage or a good pinch dried sage

1 tbsp crème fraîche (optional)

sea salt and fresh ground black pepper

1 Heat a large saucepan of lightly salted water until boiling for the pasta.

2 Meanwhile, heat half the butter with the oil in a frying pan until no longer foaming and feeling hot. Add the liver and fry for 1–2 minutes on each side until well browned and just firm when pressed with the back of a fork. Season in the pan, then remove to a warmed plate and keep warm.

3 Add the port or Madeira to the pan, bring to the boil and allow to bubble until reduced by half. Add the vinegar and cook for a few seconds. Pour in the stock and bring to the boil, stirring. Continue to boil until reduced by half.

4 Meanwhile, add the pasta to the pan of boiling water and cook for 2–3 minutes for fresh pasta or according to the packet instructions for dried pasta until just tender. Drain, then toss with the remaining butter and the fresh or dried sage.

5 Season the pasta well and divide between 2 warmed serving plates. Lay the liver over the top (you may want to slice this into attractive pieces). Whisk the crème fraîche into the sauce in the pan, if using, check the seasoning and spoon over the liver. Serve immediately.

One of the loose foods we enjoy selling are lightly sun-dried Italian tomatoes in olive oil. I call them 'sun-blushed', but their proper name is pomodorello, and they are wonderfully sweet and succulent. Serve them snipped into salads, with pasta or on pizzas or bruschetta. Alternatively, just enjoy nibbling them on their own. As this recipe reveals, I also like to use them for jazzing up pan-fried steaks.

Beef steaks with sun-blushed tomatoes and parsley

serves 2

2 beef steaks (fillet, sirloin or rump), about 200 g (7 oz) each
a good knob of butter
1 tbsp olive oil
125 g (4½ oz) pomodorello tomatoes
1 tbsp chopped fresh parsley
1 tbsp chopped fresh basil
1 tbsp balsamic vinegar
sea salt and freshly ground black pepper

1 Heat a non-stick frying pan and when you feel a good heat rising, add the steaks to the dry pan. Cook for a minute or so before adding the butter and oil. This helps to colour the steaks well.

2 After cooking for 1 minute, turn the steaks over and cook the other side. Timing depends on the thickness of the steaks and how you like them. Allow about 5 minutes in total for medium rare steaks. They should feel slightly springy when pressed with the back of a fork. Season well during cooking, then remove to warmed dinner plates.

3 Meanwhile, chop the tomatoes and place in a bowl with half the chopped herbs, the vinegar and seasoning. Add the tomato mixture to the pan and heat through for 1–2 minutes. Spoon on top of the steaks and sprinkle over the remaining herbs. Grind over black pepper and serve pronto!

the deli cookbook

Caramelized braised beef

We have become so used to eating quick-cooked beef in the form of steaks or stir-fries that we are in danger of forgetting just how delicious it can be cooked long and slow until it can be pulled apart in tender shreds. This is an easy-to-prepare dish, cooked pot-roast style. Buy the best piece of roasting beef you can afford, such as rolled sirloin, but having said that, a top rump or silverside joint will give lots of flavour if cooked for a further 30 minutes-1 hour.

serves 4

1 tbsp olive oil

1 sirloin beef joint (but *see* recipe introduction), preferably traditionally or organically reared, about 1 kg (2 lb 4 oz)

2 carrots, chopped

3 shallots, chopped

1 leek, sliced

1 tbsp caster sugar

2 fat garlic cloves, crushed

300 ml (½ pt) fresh chicken stock (buy ready-made in a tub)

300 ml (½ pt) red wine

5 tbsp balsamic vinegar

50 g (1¾ oz) butter

sea salt and freshly ground black pepper

1 Heat the oven to 180°C (350°F), Gas Mark 4. Heat the oil in a frying pan, add the beef joint and brown all over.

2 Remove the beef joint and add the vegetables, shaking the pan and stirring the vegetables to give them just a little colour.

3 Add the sugar, garlic, stock, wine, vinegar and butter to the vegetables. Bring to the boil, then transfer the vegetables and juices into a small roasting pan. Sit the beef joint on top, season well and cover loosely with a sheet of foil. Don't tuck the foil around the sides, but just shape it roughly around the outside of the joint.

4 Braise in the oven for about 1½ hours, uncovering twice during the cooking time, if possible, and spooning the pan juices over the beef.

5 Remove the meat and leave to stand for 10 minutes before carving. Serve with the caramelized vegetables and pan juices spooned over.

serving note

I like to serve this dish with a creamy risotto, topped with shavings of parmesan. You may prefer to serve it with mash.

Dishes on the side

S ome of the best meals are just plain grills or roasts served with exciting, delicious vegetable dishes or salads. In the recent past, chefs would lay great store by producing rich and heavy sauces as the key accompaniment. Now we focus instead on developing new ways of preparing root vegetables, leaves and pulses. Food today has become a whole lot more interesting and inventive – not to mention healthier!

In this section I present a few of my personal favourites which have a nice country feel to them, enlivened by a rich variety of flavourings from the deli, such as speciality vinegars and mustards; herbs and spices. One of the simplest and best dressings for vegetables is a good extra virgin olive oil, but nut oils – such as sesame, walnut or almond – are wonderfully aromatic and just a trickle is all you need to breathe life into broccoli, carrots or potatoes.

Let's not overlook the other classic accompaniment – bread. Here, I've included a couple of recipes for making your own from scratch using my recommended flour for the best results. Homemade bread is not only easy to make but offers a glorious eating experience.

Celeriac remoulade

serves 4

500 g (1 lb 2 oz) celeriac

1 red onion, thinly sliced

250 ml (9 fl oz) thick mayonnaise

3 tbsp coarse-grain mustard, eg Pommery or Gordons

grated zest and juice of 1 lemon

a dash of Worcestershire sauce

2 tbsp chopped fresh parsley

sea salt and freshly ground black pepper

This is a popular salad in France, and is sometimes sold here packed in small plastic pots. However, the homemade version is far nicer. You can serve celeriac raw, although some people prefer it blanched in boiling water for 1 minute. The sauce is a mustard mayonnaise livened up with my special touches. You can either make your own mayonnaise or use a really good-quality, ready-made one, such as the French brand Delouis Fils.

1 Peel the celeriac, then slice it as thinly as possible (use a mandolin if you have one). Stack the slices 3 or 4 at a time on top of each other and cut into long, thin julienne or matchsticks.

2 Place in a bowl and mix with the onion. (If you prefer a milder flavour, first soak the onion in a large bowl of cold water for 1 hour.)

3 Beat the mayonnaise with the mustard, lemon zest and juice, Worcestershire sauce and seasoning. Combine with the celeriac and onion. If you find the sauce a little too thick, thin it with 1–2 tbsp milk. Check the seasoning, stir in the parsley and serve in an attractive bowl.

Roast celeriac with vanilla and garlic

serves 4

1 kg (2 lb 4 oz) celeriac

1 bourbon vanilla pod (*see* ingredients note, page 115)

50 g (1¾ oz) butter, softened

4 tbsp olive oil

3 garlic cloves, unpeeled and crushed

sea salt and freshly ground black pepper

This may sound an unlikely combination of flavours, but trust me, it's delicious. Celeriac is a large, knobbly skinned, turnip-like vegetable, which is quite often sold in the major supermarkets and upmarket greengrocers. Beneath its unattractive pock-marked skin lies firm flesh with a fine fennel-like flavour.

1 Heat the oven to 180°C (350°F), Gas Mark 4. Peel the celeriac – you may find this easier to do if you first cut the vegetable into large chunks. Once peeled, cut the large chunks into smaller ones.

2 Slit the vanilla pod lengthways and with the tip of a knife scrape out the tiny seeds into the butter. Blend well.

3 Place the celeriac in a roasting pan, drizzle with the oil and dot with the vanilla-flavoured butter. Season well. Scatter around the crushed garlic cloves and add the empty vanilla pod.

4 Roast in the oven for about 40 minutes, stirring once or twice, until softened. Spoon into a warmed serving dish to serve.

serving note

This celeriac dish makes an ideal accompaniment for roasts or grilled fish.

Caramelized beetroot

serves 4

3 tbsp clear honey

25 g (1 oz) butter

4 whole cooked beetroots, cut in half

juice of 1 lemon

1 tbsp chopped fresh parsley

sea salt and freshly ground black pepper

A speedy, simple serving idea for cooked beetroot. You can use ready-cooked beets from a pack but be sure to avoid the variety contained in that awful vinegar. But better still, cook and peel your own fresh beetroot.

1 Heat a large non-stick frying pan and until you feel a good heat rising. Spoon in the honey and swirl in the butter.

2 When you have a golden brown glaze, add the beetroot halves with the lemon juice and cook for 3–5 minutes, spooning the honey juices constantly over the beetroot.

3 Season well and tip into a warmed serving dish. Scatter over the parsley and serve.

serving note

This dish is great served with roast lamb, chicken or pork.

New potato salad with truffle cream dressing

serves 4

500 g (1 lb 2 oz) small new potatoes, scrubbed

½ frisée lettuce, washed and shaken dry

125 ml (4 fl oz) double cream

juice of 1 small lemon

1 tbsp truffle oil

2 tbsp extra virgin olive oil

1 tbsp balsamic vinegar

1 tbsp chopped fresh chives

shavings from half a small black truffle (optional but well worth trying)

sea salt and freshly ground black pepper

Come May and June, baby new potatoes are at their best – full of flavour with a smooth, velvety texture. My favourite are the kidney-shaped Jersey Royals, but other parts of Britain produce excellent new spuds too – Cornwall, Pembroke, Kent and Scotland. This recipe originates from my days at the Chewton Glen Hotel in Hampshire, and is a good salad to serve as a starter. It can also be turned into a special side dish for a buffet party. The dressing is a simple blend of cream, lemon and truffle oil. Buy the best concentrated oil you can afford – it will repay you in a greater depth of flavour. But if you are really pushing the boat out, treat yourself to an actual truffle. You can buy small black ones and eke them out by slicing wafer thin on a mandolin or even a special truffle shaver. The fragrance of a fresh truffle is a waft of paradise.

1 Boil the potatoes in their skins in a saucepan of lightly salted water for about 15 minutes until tender but not overcooked. Drain well and leave to cool a little. When cool enough to handle, peel, then cut into 1 cm (½ in) slices. Season well and set aside.

2 Pick over the frisée, discarding any discoloured or damaged leaves, and tear into bite-sized pieces. Place in a bowl.

3 Whip the cream until frothy, then beat in the lemon juice (or as much as it takes to sour the cream), seasoning and the truffle oil.

4 Whisk the olive oil with the balsamic vinegar and seasoning, add to the frisée and toss well. Divide between 4 serving plates.

5 Mix the potatoes gently with the cream dressing and pile on top of the frisée. Sprinkle over the chives and season again. Scatter over the truffle slices, if using, and serve.

There was a period in the 1980s when vegetables were often served as a purée. Like all fashions, it eventually lost its appeal and purées became passé. Despite this, I like to serve meats and fish nestling on a small bed of purée. Not only does it hold them to the plate – an attribute greatly appreciated by enthusiastic waiters – but it also adds a creamy contrast to the rest of the dish. This particular recipe is another popular idea from my days working at the 190 restaurant in Queen's Gate in South Kensington, London, with my mentor, Anthony Worrall Thompson. Use Spanish butter beans, but otherwise French haricots would be a good alternative. You can make the purée in advance and simply reheat it before serving.

Butter bean and rosemary purée

serves 4

175 g (6 oz) dried white beans (*see* recipe introduction)

1 tbsp olive oil

3 shallots, chopped

3 fat garlic cloves, crushed

3 rashers of smoked bacon or pancetta, rinded and chopped

leaves stripped from 1 sprig of fresh rosemary, chopped

1 sprig of fresh thyme

150 ml (¼ pt) dry white wine

400 ml (14 fl oz) fresh chicken or vegetable stock (buy ready-made in a tub)

2–4 tbsp double cream or crème fraîche

sea salt and freshly ground black pepper

1 Soak the beans in water overnight, then drain and rinse. Place in a saucepan, cover with cold water and bring to the boil. Continue to boil for 5 minutes, then drain.

2 Meanwhile, heat the oil in a frying pan, add the shallots, garlic and bacon or pancetta and sauté for 5 minutes. Add the blanched beans with the rosemary, thyme, wine and stock. Bring to the boil, then season with pepper only.

3 Cover and simmer for about 30 minutes until the beans are softened. Remove the lid, add salt to season and boil again to evaporate any remaining liquid. Remove the thyme sprig and transfer the bean mixture to a food processor or blender. Add the cream or crème fraîche and whizz to a purée.

variation

You can make a quicker version of this dish using 2 x 400 g (14 oz) cans butter beans in place of the dried beans. Simply rinse and drain the beans, then add them to the sautéed shallots, garlic and bacon or pancetta with the herbs and wine, but without the stock. Simmer for 15 minutes, then blend with the cream or crème fraîche to make a purée.

Olive focaccia with rosemary oil

Bread-making is easy and can be deeply satisfying, so why not try your hand at making focaccia? This recipe makes two loaves, one of which you could freeze for later use.

makes 2 loaves, approximately 20cm (8in) in diameter

500g (1lb 2oz) bread flour, ideally Italian Tipo 2 (*see* ingredients notes)

1 sachet easy-blend yeast

½ tsp sea salt

½ tsp caster sugar

300ml (½ pt) olive oil

300ml (½ pt) tepid water

2 large sprigs of fresh rosemary

60g (2¼oz) pitted black olives, chopped

sea salt flakes, for sprinkling (*see* ingredients notes)

1 It is easier to make the bread in an electric mixer with a dough hook, or in a strong food processor. Sift the flour, yeast, salt and sugar into the mixer or food processor bowl. Alternatively, sift the flour, yeast, salt and sugar into a large mixing bowl.

2 Add 2 tbsp of the oil. Gradually mix in the water until a soft but not too sticky dough forms, with the machine running on a slow speed or using your hands. You may not need all the water, or you may need extra, so add with care. Continue to beat for 5–10 minutes until the dough is smooth and elastic or knead the dough on a lightly floured surface for about 10 minutes.

3 Place the dough in a lightly oiled bowl and cover loosely with clingfilm, allowing room for expansion. Leave to rise (prove) in a warm place (such as an airing cupboard or near a central-heating boiler) until doubled in size. This can take 30 minutes or up to 2 hours, depending on how warm it is.

4 Meanwhile, heat the remaining oil gently in a small saucepan and add the rosemary. Remove the pan from the heat and leave to allow the flavour to infuse.

5 Knock back the dough by punching it down with your fist and knead by hand on a lightly floured surface for a few minutes. Divide in half and shape into 2 rounds about 1.5cm (⅝ in) thick.

6 Place each round on a lightly greased baking sheet and cover loosely with clingfilm. Leave to prove for about 20–30 minutes until doubled in size. Meanwhile, heat the oven to 200°C (400°F), Gas Mark 6.

7 Make small indentations with your fingers all over the surface of each loaf. Brush with the rosemary oil, scatter over the olives and sprinkle with sea salt flakes. Bake for 20 minutes until risen and golden brown. Cool on a wire rack.

ingredients notes

Track down the special wheat flour known as Tipo 2, a medium-ground, unbleached flour (makes wonderful pizzas, too). Sea salt flakes are a must to create the characteristic crust; I would recommend Maldon as the best brand.

serving note

Either tear the focaccia into pieces or cut into wedges. Serve with any remaining rosemary oil, which you can strain if you like, for dipping. Bellissimo!

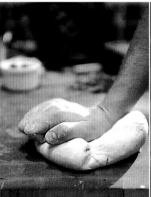

Roasted garlic and olive oil bread

I believe in letting guests help themselves when they come to my home. It makes life easier for me and the evening more relaxing for everyone. This is wonderful food for guests (and host) to nibble while waiting for the rest of the meal to appear. You'll need a couple or more deliciously flavoured loaves of crusty bread, such as walnut or sun-dried tomato, cumin seed or onion.

serves 6–8

6–8 whole large heads of garlic
250 ml (9 fl oz) olive oil
3–4 sprigs of fresh thyme
2–3 loaves of assorted flavoured breads
sea salt flakes (*see* ingredients notes, page 76)

1 Heat the oven to 190°C (375°F), Gas Mark 5. Cut the garlic heads in half widthways and lay on a baking sheet. Drizzle over the oil. Strip the leaves from the thyme sprigs and scatter over the garlic with some crushed salt flakes.

2 Roast in the oven for about 15–20 minutes until the garlic flesh feels soft when pierced with the tip of a knife.

3 Meanwhile, slice the breads of your choice. If you have time and the facilities for grilling, ie a large barbecue or grill pan, you can chargrill the slices and serve as toast.

4 Transfer the garlic to a serving plate and let your guests scoop out the soft sweet flesh to spread on the bread or toast.

serving note

You can also serve bowls of extra virgin olive oil and pots of sea salt to sprinkle over the garlic-spread bread or toast.

I had often seen butternut squashes with their pretty apricot-coloured skins and lightbulb shapes in food stores, but it took a contestant in one of my early *Ready, Steady, Cook* shows to prompt me to cook it for the first time. Inspiration and imagination were on my side on that show, and the resulting recipe is one that I've used often ever since.

Roast butternut squash with lemon and mustard

serves 4–6

2 butternut squash, about 650 g (1 lb 7 oz) each

2 garlic cloves, crushed

grated zest and juice of 2 lemons

1 tbsp olive oil

90 g (3¼ oz) butter, 60 g (2¼ oz) melted, remainder lightly chilled

leaves stripped from 1 sprig of fresh thyme

2–3 tbsp coarse-grain mustard, eg Pommery or Gordons

5 tbsp double cream

sea salt and freshly ground black pepper

1 Heat the oven to 190°C (375°F), Gas Mark 5. Cut the squash in half, scoop out the seeds, then peel and chop the flesh into evenly sized chunks. Place in a bowl and add the garlic, lemon zest and juice, oil and half the melted butter.

2 Toss the ingredients together, then spread out in a roasting pan. Scatter over the thyme leaves and roast in the oven for about 20 minutes until the squash feels tender when pierced with the tip of a knife.

3 Scoop the roasted squash into a food processor or blender with the remaining melted butter, mustard, cream and seasoning. Whizz to a smooth purée, spoon into a serving dish and dot with the chilled butter.

serving note

A perfect accompaniment to roasted meats.

variation

This recipe also works well using sweet potato in place of the butternut squash.

dishes on the side

79

Fresh leaf pasta

This is a good bit of fun – and tasty as well, fresh herbs rolled into freshly made pasta. Making your own pasta is simple if you have one of those hand cranked pasta machines. It helps too if you have the right sort of flour. A good deli that specialises in Italian foods will stock a flour called 00 or doppio zero (strong bread flour makes tough fresh pasta). Cut the pasta into small rounds, thick strips or use in sheets for an elegant lasagne. You can make the pasta with whole leaf herbs, chopped herbs or, of course, with no herbs at all.

serves 2–3

275 g (9½ oz) pasta flour
1 tsp salt
1 tbsp olive oil
2 egg yolks
2 medium eggs, beaten
a selection of whole fresh herb leaves, eg thyme, sage, coriander or mint

1 Put the flour and salt (and chopped herbs, if using instead of whole leaf) into a food processor. With the blades running, drop in the oil, yolks and most of the beaten eggs.

2 Blend the mixture until it just starts to stick together (you can check on this if you press a little together between your fingers). You may not need all the egg – it depends on the flour. If you use all the egg and it still seems a little dry, trickle in some cold water. Do not overbeat the dough, just pull it together into a ball.

3 Set up your pasta machine. Break off a lump of dough the size of a large walnut and with the rollers set on the highest number, feed the dough through about five times.

4 Set the rollers to the next setting down and repeat. Repeat this until you reach the third thinnest setting. By now the dough will have become very smooth and elastic. Try and keep the edges as straight as possible.

5 Lay the dough sheet out on a lightly floured board, and if using whole herb leaves press them lightly on to the dough (see method steps below).

6 Repeat with the remaining dough in stages. After rolling out the second sheet, place this on top of the first and press down. Feed this double sheet through the rollers again. Keep on rolling and pressing the leaves in until finished.

7 Cut the pasta into rounds or straight sheets and leave to dry on sheets of non-stick baking parchment.

8 Blanch in a large pan of salted boiling water for just 1–2 minutes until al dente.

9 Serve the pasta dressed with butter and grated parmesan.

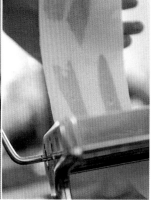

Bubble and squeak cakes

I love a fry-up, and this is simply a more elegant way of serving the classic, ever-popular 'bubble and squeak'.

makes 4

500g (1 lb 2oz) floury potatoes, eg king edward, maris piper or desirée, peeled and chopped

125g (4½oz) shredded green cabbage

olive or sunflower oil, for frying

3 rashers smoked bacon, rinded and chopped

1 shallot, chopped

2 garlic cloves, crushed

3 tbsp chopped mixed fresh herbs, eg parsley, dill or coriander

seasoned flour, for coating

sea salt and freshly ground black pepper

1 Boil the potatoes in lightly salted water for about 15 minutes until just tender, then drain well and mash in the pan. Leave in the pan.

2 Blanch the cabbage in a little boiling water for 2 minutes, then drain, rinse under cold running water and pat dry with kitchen paper.

3 Heat a trickle of oil in a frying pan, add the bacon and fry until crisp. Remove and drain on kitchen paper. Add 1 tbsp of oil to the pan, add the shallot and garlic and sauté for 3 minutes until softened.

4 Add the shallot and garlic to the mashed potato with the cabbage, bacon, chopped herbs and seasoning. Set aside to cool.

5 Shape the mixture into 4 cakes. Toss in seasoned flour to coat, shaking off any excess. Heat oil to a depth of 1 cm (½ in) in a large frying pan. Lower the cakes into the hot oil using a fish slice and cook for about 3 minutes on each side, turning them carefully. Remove and drain on kitchen paper.

serving note

These delicious cakes can be served with all sorts of dishes, from the sophisticated Pepper-crusted monkfish with mustard dill sauce, page 45, to a humble plate of eggs and bacon.

This is a great party bread which you can serve freshly baked and sliced, spread with a good garlic soft cheese or lashings of fresh unsalted butter. It is especially good with seafood barbecues.

When I was a student chef, our college group was sent to work at various restaurants in the Pornic area of the South of France. We knew when we returned to Yorkshire that we would each have to cook a speciality of the region where we had worked, so before we left we all packed whatever special ingredients were needed to take home. Some packed vine twigs, but I took back a sack of T45 flour used by French bakers in the making of their superb bread. What none of us had anticipated was that when our minibus went through Customs, the officers viewed a bus-load of scruffy students with great suspicion. We were held while they examined our hash-like vine twigs and stabbed at my sack with its sinister-looking contents of white powder.

Eventually, we made it back to our college kitchens and I made a bread very much like this one with that T45 flour. It's a firm favourite now.

Smoked salmon and basil bread

makes 1 x 1kg (2lb 4oz) loaf

250g (9oz) French or Italian bread flour eg T45 or Tipo 2 (*see* ingredients notes, page 76)

250g (9oz) strong white flour, plus extra for dusting (alternatively, use 500g/1lb 2oz of one of the above flours)

½ tsp sea salt

either 15g (½oz) fresh yeast or 1 sachet easy-blend yeast

a good pinch of sugar, if using fresh yeast

1 tbsp olive oil, plus extra, for greasing

200ml (7 floz) tepid milk

5 tbsp tepid water

150g (5½oz) smoked salmon, chopped (you could use trimmings)

4 large leaves fresh basil, chopped

1 Sift the flours (or flour) and salt together into a large bowl. If using fresh yeast, cream with 2 tbsp of the milk, the sugar and 1 tsp of the flour. Leave until it starts to froth. If using the easy-blend yeast, simply stir into the flour.

2 Blend the oil with the milk and water. Beat the creamed yeast, if using, into the flour, then gradually work in the oil and milk mixture until you have a soft but not too sticky dough. You may not need all the liquid, or you may need to add extra tepid water in cautious dribbles – it all depends on the flour.

3 Work the dough vigorously with your hands until it leaves the side of the bowl, then turn it out on to a lightly floured surface. Knead it back and forth using a scrubbing action, scrunching the dough into a ball and kneading time and time again. It will begin to get smoother and more elastic after 5–10 minutes.

4 Place the dough in a lightly oiled bowl and cover with loosely with clingfilm, allowing room for expansion. Leave to rise (prove) in a warm place (such as an airing cupboard or near a central-heating boiler) until the dough is doubled in size.

5 Knock back the dough by punching it with your fist. Knead on a lightly floured surface, gradually working in the smoked salmon and basil with your hands. Shape the dough into a long oval and place it on a lightly oiled non-stick baking sheet. Score 3 slashes in the top and lightly dust with flour.

6 Cover loosely again with clingfilm and leave to prove a second time for about 1 hour until doubled in size. Meanwhile, heat the oven to 190°C (375°F), Gas Mark 5.

7 Bake the dough for 30–35 minutes until firm on the outside and cooked inside. You can check this by turning the loaf over and knocking the base – it should sound hollow. If it makes a dull thud instead, bake for a further 5 minutes or so.

8 Cool on a wire rack. When cold, slice and enjoy – real, fresh homemade bread with a wonderful salmon flavour.

One course meals

Meal times are a-changing. The formal three-course dinner has given way to a more informal, relaxed style of serving and eating a meal. The recipes in this chapter have been created as all-in-one, light main courses to suit this growing trend towards bistro-style or alfresco eating, dispensing with the need for separate serving dishes and accompaniments, except perhaps for a crunchy salad or a hunk of crusty bread to mop up the last of a delicious sauce or a trickle of oil. Many are even cooked in one pot or on one oven tray, making them ultra-convenient to prepare as well as to serve.

Several of the dishes are Mediterranean in flavour and texture, for example the risottos. I adore this Italian classic because while the basic ingredients generally remain the same – rice, garlic, onions, oil and stock – the extra ingredients you then add give the dish its unique individuality.

Pastas are the best-loved one-course meals, and there are just so many pasta shapes and sizes to choose from. If you feel somewhat bewildered as you stand in front of the deli shelves stacked with pasta, just remember that flat pasta suits thin sauces or a light dressing of oil or pesto, while pasta with tubes or pockets are intended for thicker more creamy sauces that nestle in the hollows.

Pizzas and their crusty cousins, bruschettas, make a few ingredients go even further and have the advantage of being ideal to eat even without a fork – perfect for party food.

Red onion and crème fraîche pizzas

serves 4

225 g (8 oz) plain flour
3 tbsp rye flour
a good pinch of sea salt
1 sachet easy-blend yeast
1 tbsp olive oil
about 100 ml (3½ fl oz) tepid water

On occasions, it's well worth making your own pizza base from scratch and keeping the topping simple and delicious. Easy-blend or fast-action yeasts are sold in easy-to-use sachets that you mix straight into flour. This gives you the best of both worlds – a wonderful homemade bread base made in next to no time. Here, the base is given a hip Californian sourdough flavour with the addition of a little rye flour. The pizza is then baked with whole garlic cloves which you can squeeze over the hot and bubbling pizza before you devour it.

topping

25 g (1 oz) butter
2 tbsp olive oil, plus extra, for drizzling
3 large red onions, thinly sliced
250 g (9 oz) full-fat crème fraîche (half-fat is too runny)
6 fat garlic cloves, peeled
4 sprigs of fresh thyme
sea salt and freshly ground black pepper

1 Heat the oven to 200°C (400°F), Gas Mark 6. Sift the flours and salt into a large bowl and stir in the yeast. Mix in the oil, then gradually add the water until you have a firm but sticky dough.

2 Turn the dough out on to a lightly floured surface. Knead well for about 5 minutes until it becomes smooth and elastic. Cover the dough loosely with clingfilm and set aside while you prepare the topping.

3 Heat the butter with the oil in a frying pan, add the onions and sauté for a good 10 minutes until softened. Leave to cool a little.

4 Divide the dough into 2 rounds. Roll each round out on a lightly floured surface as thinly as possible – they should be 25–30 cm (10–12 in) in diameter. Place on lightly greased baking sheets.

5 Spread the dough tops with the crème fraîche, then cover with the onions and season well. Press 3 whole garlic cloves on top of each pizza and strip the leaves from thyme sprigs over the top. Drizzle with a little more olive oil.

6 Bake in the oven for about 15–20 minutes until golden brown. Serve hot and bubbling from the oven, squeezing the soft flesh from the garlic cloves over the top of the pizza.

This is the sort of dish you could pay serious money for in a restaurant, but is in fact quite easy to put together. You bake sliced aubergines and buffalo mozzarella in layers, sprinkled in between with a classic Italian gremolata – a blend of parsley, garlic and lemon. Serve with a homemade spicy tomato sauce, but if time is short, a good ready-made tomato sauce rich in oil and garlic will stand in for the homemade version.

Aubergine and mozzarella stacks

serves 4

2 large aubergines, sliced 1 cm (½ in) thick

olive oil, for brushing

1 mugful of fresh flat leaf parsley

3 garlic cloves, finely chopped

grated zest of 1 lemon

1 tsp chopped fresh rosemary

4 balls buffalo mozzarella, about 100 g (3½ oz) each

sea salt and freshly ground black pepper

sauce

1 tbsp olive oil

1 shallot, finely chopped

1 small plump fresh red chilli, deseeded and chopped

1 garlic clove, finely chopped

8 ripe plum tomatoes, skinned and chopped

a good pinch of sugar

2 tbsp chopped fresh basil

1 Heat the oven to 180°C (350°F), Gas Mark 4. Brush the aubergine slices with oil and season lightly. Heat a ridged griddle pan until you feel a good heat rising. Add the aubergine slices and chargrill for about 3 minutes on each side until softened. You need to do this in batches. Remove and leave to cool.

2 To make the gremolata, finely chop the parsley sprigs and mix with the garlic, lemon zest and rosemary.

3 Cut the balls of mozzarella into 1 cm (½ in) slices. Divide the mozzarella and aubergine slices into 4 equal portions. Layer the slices alternately on a lightly greased baking sheet, sprinkling the gremolata and seasoning between each layer, to make 4 stacks, 4–5 layers high, using the larger pieces for the bases and the smaller pieces on top.

4 Bake the stacks in the oven for about 15 minutes until the cheese just starts to melt.

5 Meanwhile, to make the sauce, heat the oil in a frying pan, add the shallot, chilli and garlic and sauté for about 5 minutes. Add the chopped tomatoes, sugar and seasoning. Cook for about 10 minutes until you have a thick sauce, stirring occasionally. Add the basil, then leave to cool. Transfer to a food processor or blender and process to make a purée. Reheat the sauce in a clean saucepan and keep warm.

6 Place each stack in the centre of a warmed serving plate with the sauce spooned alongside.

Anchovy and rosemary pizzas

serves 2

1 medium-sized pizza
base or medium-sized
ciabatta

300g (10½oz) jar tomato
pasta sauce (any flavour)

2 x 150g (5½oz) packs
buffalo mozzarella

1 large sprig of fresh
rosemary

1 x 50g (1¾oz) can salted
anchovies,
drained if in oil

4 tbsp freshly grated
parmesan

freshly ground
black pepper

Packet pizzas often taste rather artificial. However, making your own from scratch can take a lot of time. The compromise is to use ready-made pizza bases. Failing that, use a ciabatta bread which you can split in two. For the topping, choose a homestyle tomato sauce. I like to use one made by the Bay Tree Food Company, but there are some authentic Italian pasta sauces that can double as pizza spreads. Be sure to use buffalo mozzarella for a fine flavour.

1 Heat the oven to 200°C (400°F), Gas Mark 6. Place the pizza base on a large baking sheet. If using ciabatta, split in half widthways with a bread knife and open it up into 2 halves.

2 Spread the pizza base or ciabatta with the tomato sauce, taking it right up to the edges. Drain the mozzarella, cut into thin slices and arrange over the tomato sauce.

3 Strip the leaves from the rosemary sprig and snip into small pieces using kitchen scissors.

Sprinkle the rosemary over the mozzarella. Layer the anchovy fillets on top, as artistically as you like or simply position them at random, then sprinkle over half the parmesan.

4 Grind over some pepper and bake in the oven for 10–15 minutes until the cheese starts to bubble. Serve with the remaining parmesan sprinkled over. Eat when piping hot and most delicious.

Grilled gravadlax with pesto gnocchi

serves 2

250g (9oz) pack
ready-made gnocchi

2 knobs of butter

125g (4½oz) freshly
made pesto (see
ingredients note)

250g (9oz) gravadlax

olive oil, for brushing

sea salt and freshly
ground black pepper

This is so easy to make, it's almost embarrassing. You can pick up the ingredients from your neighbourhood deli on your way home from work and knock up a meal almost instantly – a boon when you are tired and hungry after a long, hard day.

1 Cook the gnocchi in a saucepan of lightly salted boiling water according to the packet instructions until just tender. Drain and toss with the butter. Return the gnocchi to the cooking pan and stir in the pesto.

2 Heat the pan and cook the gnocchi in the pesto for about 2–3 minutes. Season and keep warm.

3 Meanwhile, heat the grill until hot. Lay the slices of gravadlax on the grill rack, brush lightly with oil and place under the hot grill for a few minutes until it turns light pink and just starts to turn brown.

4 Tip the gnocchi into 2 warmed wide serving bowls and drape the cooked gravadlax over the top. Grind over black pepper and serve.

ingredients note

Ideally, buy freshly made pesto, but otherwise, a good rule of thumb is to look for pesto in a jar with the darkest colour you can find. This indicates that plenty of aromatic, fresh basil has been used.

Mussel and artichoke risotto

serves 3–4

1 kg (2 lb 4 oz) fresh mussels (*see* ingredients note)

3 garlic cloves, crushed

3 shallots or 1 onion, chopped

150 ml (¼ pt) dry white wine

50 g (1¾ oz) butter

2 tbsp olive oil

400 g (14 oz) Jerusalem artichokes, peeled and finely chopped

250 g (9 oz) risotto rice (arborio or carnaroli)

about 800 ml (1 pt 7 fl oz) fresh fish stock or chicken stock (buy ready-made in a tub)

2 tbsp mascarpone

3 tbsp freshly grated parmesan

1 tbsp chopped fresh parsley

sea salt and freshly ground black pepper

Both mussels and artichokes are warming wintry comfort foods, so this risotto is ideal for when you just want to curl up in front of an open fire. Cook the mussels first in a little wine and butter until they open, then pull out the meat from the shells. It takes just minutes to prepare.

1 Wash the mussels in cold water, then pull away the wispy 'beards'. Place the mussels in a large pan but discard any that are open. Add 1 crushed garlic clove, 1 chopped shallot or one-third of the chopped onion, the wine and half the butter.

2 Cover with a tight lid and cook over a medium heat for about 7 minutes. Uncover, strain the juices into a jug and set aside. When the mussels are cool enough to handle, pull the meat from the shells and set aside. Discard any mussels that have not opened.

3 Heat the oil in a frying pan, add the remaining garlic, shallots or onion and artichokes and gently sauté for about 5 minutes until softened.

4 Stir in the rice and cook for 1–2 minutes until lightly toasted, then pour in all the mussel juices. Bring to the boil, stirring, and cook for about 5 minutes until the liquid is absorbed, stirring frequently.

5 Heat the stock until simmering and add a quarter to the rice. Simmer, uncovered, until the stock is absorbed, stirring frequently. Add the remainder of the stock a ladleful at a time in the same way until all the stock is absorbed and the rice grains are plump and tender yet still retain a good 'bite'. This should take 15–18 minutes. You may not need all the stock.

6 Stir in the mussels, the remaining butter, mascarpone, parmesan and parsley. Season well and serve piping hot and creamy.

ingredients note

Irish and French mussels are the best ones to look out for. They are grown on ropes clear of the sandy sea bottom, so remain free of grit.

2 red mullet fillets, about
200 g (7 oz) each, skin on

1 head of chicory, hard
core removed and leaves
separated

a good handful of fresh
rocket leaves

2 fresh plum tomatoes,
deseeded

25 g (1 oz) parmesan

2 tbsp olive oil

4 small chargrilled red
peppers in oil from
a jar, drained

sea salt and freshly
ground black pepper

dressing
4 tbsp olive oil

juice of 1 lemon

1 tbsp balsamic vinegar

1 small shallot,
finely chopped

1 tsp truffle oil (optional,
but effective)

Brindisa Foods import the most divine ready-grilled and skinned baby red peppers from Spain, which I use in a quick dish of pan-fried red mullet served on a chicory-leaf salad. Tucked in between are shavings of sweet, tangy parmesan and the whole plate is drizzled with a truffle-flavoured lemon-and-oil dressing.

Mullet on smoky red pepper salad

1 Check the mullet for any stray bones by running your fingers along the flesh. If you feel any, pinch them out with your fingertips or use a pair of tweezers. Set the fish aside.

2 Tear the chicory leaves into bite-sized pieces and mix with the rocket in a bowl. Slice the tomatoes and add to the bowl with seasoning.

3 Whisk together all the ingredients for the dressing. Shave the parmesan into slivers using a swivel vegetable peeler.

4 Heat the oil in a large frying pan, add the mullet, skin side down, and cook for about 5 minutes until the flesh feels just firm when pressed with the back of a fork. Carefully turn over with a fish slice, taking care not to damage the pretty pink skin. Cook the flesh side very briefly – 1 minute at the most.

5 Toss the salad with half the dressing. Divide between serving plates and place in the centre of each. Top with the parmesan shavings, then 2 peppers each and finally crown with the mullet fillets, skin side up (the skin is so inviting, why not flaunt it?). Drizzle the remainder of the dressing around the plates in a swirl and serve.

One of my little 'cheats' is to dress up a carton of Campbell's' Deliciously Good soup, which can keep for weeks without the need for refrigeration yet tastes as fresh and delicious as homemade. The carrot and coriander variety makes a great instant sauce for a seafood platter, spiked with some freshly roasted cumin seeds. You will need a selection – or mèlange as chefs would term it – of neatly prepared fresh fish and seafood.

Seafood pot

serves 2

4 king scallops with corals, prepared

1 tsp cumin seeds

2 tbsp olive oil

a knob of butter

1 red mullet fillet, about 125 g (4½ oz), halved

1 monkfish fillet, about 125 g (4½ oz), cut into 2 medallions

1 sea bass or brill fillet, about 125 g (4½ oz), halved

1 salmon fillet, about 125 g (4½ oz), halved

4 baby or 1 medium-sized squid, cut into rings

a wedge of lemon, for squeezing

250 ml (9 fl oz) carton Campbell's' Deliciously Good Carrot and Coriander Soup

1 tbsp chopped fresh coriander

sea salt and freshly ground black pepper

1 Check that the scallops have been thoroughly cleaned and remove any thin black threads. Pat dry with kitchen paper.

2 Heat a large non-stick frying pan, add the cumin seeds and dry-roast for about 3–4 minutes, tossing in the pan. Tip straight into a pestle and mortar and grind until quite finely ground.

3 Add 1 tbsp of oil and butter to the pan. When hot, add the fish and fry quickly until just cooked. The flesh of the fish should be well browned and the skin crispy.

4 Heat a griddle pan and add the remaining oil. Add the scallops and squid and cook quickly – squid must not be overcooked or they will be tough.

5 Remove the fish and seafood to a dish to keep warm. Season well and squeeze over a little lemon juice.

6 Pour the soup into the pan and add the ground cumin. Heat until gently bubbling and continue to simmer for about 2 minutes. Pour into warmed shallow soup bowls. Arrange the fish and seafood on top and scatter over the coriander. Serve immediately.

Crab cakes

Fish cakes are versatile little things. They can be homely and simple or wildly sophisticated. They can also be very dry and stodgy, but not this recipe. Make them ahead and serve with a homemade relish, such as my Cucumber and green pepper relish, page 137, or buy a good-quality relish if you haven't the time or inclination. If you can't find fresh dressed crab meat, then frozen or a superior branded can of white meat will do.

serves 4

500 g (1 lb 2 oz) king edward potatoes, peeled and cut into large, evenly sized chunks

25 g (1 oz) butter

2 tbsp double cream

1 tsp mild or medium-strength curry powder

2 tbsp chopped fresh coriander

1 large fresh green chilli, deseeded and finely chopped

1 tbsp grated red onion

500 g (1 lb 2 oz) flaked crab meat, preferably white meat but a mixture of white and brown will do, thawed well if frozen

2–3 tbsp plain flour, seasoned

2 medium free-range eggs, beaten

100 g (3½ oz) dried breadcrumbs (uncoloured)

corn or sunflower oil, for deep frying

sea salt and freshly ground black pepper

1 Boil the potatoes in a saucepan of lightly salted water for about 15 minutes until tender. Drain well, then return to the pan. Mash with a fork or potato masher until smooth, beating in the butter, cream, curry powder, coriander, chilli, onion and lots of seasoning. Leave to cool completely.

2 Meanwhile, check the crab meat carefully for any flecks of shell and discard. Mix the crab meat with the potato mixture, then shape into 8 neat round patties. If the mixture sticks to your hands, simply dip them in cold water.

3 To coat the crab cakes in breadcrumbs requires a methodical approach. Complete each of the 3 stages for all the cakes before moving on to the next. That way, you won't get too messy. So, first toss each cake in seasoned flour, shake well and place on a plate.

4 Beat the eggs in a wide shallow bowl, then dip each cake into the egg to coat evenly.

5 Place the breadcrumbs in another wide shallow bowl and toss each cake in the crumbs in turn, pressing the crumbs on to the eggy surface to coat evenly. Shake off any excess and place on a plate. Chill in the refrigerator for about 30 minutes to 'set' the crumbs.

6 Heat oil to a depth of 1 cm (½ in) in a wide shallow frying pan until you feel a good heat rising. Carefully slide in the crab cakes using a fish slice. Cook for about 3 minutes until crisp and golden brown on the underside, then carefully turn and cook the other side. Remove and place on kitchen paper. (If you have a medium-sized frying pan, you may find it best to fry the crab cakes in 2 batches.) Serve piping hot. However, if not serving immediately, place uncovered in a warm oven so that the coating stays crisp.

1 tbsp olive oil

175 g (6 oz) good-quality
black pudding, cut into
thick slices, then
into quarters

1 smoked Finnan haddock
fillet, about 300–400 g
(10½–14 oz)

25 g (1 oz) butter

3 shallots, chopped

2 garlic cloves, crushed

100 ml (3½ fl oz) dry
white wine

250 g (9 oz) risotto rice
(arborio or carnaroli)

about 1.2 l (2 pts) fresh
fish or vegetable stock
(buy ready-made in a tub)

2 medium leeks,
thinly sliced

2–3 tbsp mascarpone or
crème fraîche

freshly grated parmesan
(to taste)

chopped fresh parsley,
to garnish

sea salt and freshly
ground black pepper

You need the real Finnan haddock with its creamy golden flesh for this recipe, not the bright yellow artificially dyed fish that masquerades as smoked fish. Good smoked haddock is naturally coloured through the smoking process. The fish itself is plump and moist with a wonderful salty-sweet flavour from the simple, pure brine. I like to mix flakes of this fish into a leek risotto, and as a surprise, toss in a few cubes of crisply fried black pudding. Not only does it tastes amazing, it looks so appealing. Try it for a light supper or unusual starter.

Leek and haddock risotto

1 Heat the oil in a wide shallow pan, add the chunks of black pudding and fry quickly for 1–2 minutes until crisp on the outside. Remove and set aside.

2 Skin the haddock and check carefully for any bones by running against the grain of the flesh with your fingertips. If you find any, pluck them out with your fingers or use a pair of tweezers. Cut the fish into 1 cm (½ in) chunks and set aside.

3 Heat the butter in the wide shallow pan, add the shallots and garlic and sauté for about 3 minutes until softened. Pour in the wine, bring to the boil and cook until reduced by half, stirring frequently. Stir in the rice and cook for 1–2 minutes until lightly toasted.

4 Heat the stock until simmering and add a quarter to the rice. Simmer, uncovered, until the stock is absorbed, stirring frequently.

5 Add a further quarter of the stock with the leeks and continue simmering until the liquid is absorbed, stirring occasionally. Add the fish, black pudding, the remaining stock and seasoning to taste. Continue simmering, stirring occasionally, until most of the stock is absorbed and the rice grains are plump and tender yet still retain a good 'bite'. The fish should be just cooked. The whole process should take 15–18 minutes.

6 Stir in the mascarpone or crème fraîche and parmesan. Check the seasoning and serve immediately, sprinkled with chopped parsley.

one course meals

Lemon-dressed pasta with chargrilled salmon

serves 4

500 g (1 lb 2 oz) good-quality pasta tubes, eg ferrazzudi di caladria, giant rigatoni or flat pappardelle

4 salmon escalopes or fillets, about 100 g (3½ oz) each, skin removed

3 tbsp olive oil

grated zest and juice of 1 large lemon

50 g (1¾ oz) butter

3–4 tbsp double cream or crème fraîche

4 tbsp chopped mixed fresh herbs, eg basil, parsley, oregano or dill

50 g (1¾ oz) parmesan freshly grated

sea salt and freshly ground black pepper

It is always worth buying the best pasta you can afford. It will reward you in flavour and texture. Generally speaking, I would suggest you steer clear of multi-coloured gimmicky shaped pasta, but there are a few varieties that I consider to be exceptions to the rule. One of these is ferrazzudi di caladria – huge tubes of subtly coloured pasta. If you can't find this particular pasta, large rigatoni tubes would do, or even flat, thick pappardelle 'noodles'. This dish makes an excellent light summer-style lunch.

1 Cook the pasta in a large saucepan of lightly salted boiling water for about 10 minutes, or according to the packet instructions, until just tender. Drain and tip straight into a large bowl.

2 Brush the salmon lightly with 1 tbsp of the oil, season and set aside while you finish the pasta.

3 Add the lemon zest and juice to the pasta with the remaining oil, butter, cream or crème fraîche, herbs, parmesan and seasoning. Mix well and set aside.

4 Heat a ridged griddle pan until you feel a good heat rising, or heat the grill until hot. Add the salmon escalopes or fillets to the griddle pan, or place under the grill, and cook for 2–3 minutes on each side. (They should be neatly marked in chargrilled ridges if cooked in the pan.) The flesh inside should be lightly pink. Divide the pasta between warmed wide shallow serving bowls or plates, top with the salmon and grind over some black pepper.

Charred smoked halibut and saffron risotto

serves 4

1 l (1¾ pt) fresh fish stock (buy ready-made in a tub)

a good pinch or two of saffron strands (*see* ingredients note)

1 tbsp olive oil, plus extra, for brushing

25 g (1 oz) butter

2 shallots, finely chopped

2 garlic cloves, chopped

250 g (9 oz) risotto rice (arborio or carnaroli)

250 g (9 oz) smoked halibut slices

1 tbsp chopped fresh dill

40 g (1½ oz) parmesan, freshly grated

sea salt and freshly ground black pepper

Smoked halibut has a lovely delicate texture and pretty golden and creamy tasting flesh. It makes a good substitute for smoked salmon as a starter, or try it lightly chargrilled and served with a risotto cooked in the classic Milano style with saffron and parmesan.

1 Pour the stock into a saucepan and bring to the boil. Remove from the heat and add the saffron. Leave to infuse while you make the risotto.

2 Heat the oil with the butter in a frying pan, add the shallots and garlic and sauté for about 5 minutes until softened. Stir in the rice and cook for 1–2 minutes until the grains are lightly toasted.

3 Heat the stock until simmering and add a quarter to the rice. Simmer, uncovered, until the stock is absorbed, stirring frequently. Add the remainder of the stock a ladleful at a time in the same way until all the stock is absorbed and the rice grains are plump and tender yet still retain a good 'bite'.

This should take 15–18 minutes. You may not need all the stock.

4 Meanwhile, heat a ridged griddle pan and brush lightly with a tiny amount of oil. When hot, lay the halibut slices in the pan and cook for 1–2 minutes until marked on only one side. Don't overcook.

5 Season the risotto to taste and stir in the dill. Spoon into warmed serving bowls and sprinkle over the parmesan. Lay the halibut slices on top and serve immediately.

ingredients note

Buy a good-quality Spanish brand of saffron with a deep aroma. You only need a pinch or two to impart a fine flavour.

There's now a good range of tortellini – those stuffed morsels of pasta in a range of flavours and colours – to be found in delis, both fresh and dried. I prefer chicken or salmon tortellini, but you could use any of the cheese or spinach varieties in this recipe. Cèpes (called porcini in Italy) are a species of wild mushroom, the Boletus edulis, and a cook's very good friend. Sold dried in handy packs, they keep almost indefinitely yet when soaked yield a great flavour. You can use the soaking broth, too, as an almost instant stock.

Tortellini in a cèpes sauce

serves 4

40 g (1½ oz) dried cèpes or porcini pieces

300 ml (½ pt) boiling water

1 tbsp olive oil

2 shallots, chopped

2 cloves garlic, crushed

2 tbsp brandy

100 ml (3½ fl oz) muscat wine or other sweet white wine

250 ml (9 fl oz) double cream

400 g (14 oz) tortellini, chicken, fish, cheese or spinach filling, fresh or dried

4 tbsp chopped fresh herbs, eg dill, parsley or chervil, plus a few whole sprigs, to garnish

a good knob of butter

2–3 tsp truffle oil (*see* ingredients note)

sea salt and freshly ground black pepper

1 Place the dried *cèpes* in a bowl and pour over the boiling water to just cover. Cover the bowl and leave for 5 minutes. Drain, but reserve the soaking liquid. Slice the cèpes if large and set aside.

2 Heat the oil in a frying pan, add the shallots and garlic and sauté for about 5 minutes until softened. Stir in the brandy and wine. Bring to the boil and cook until reduced by half.

3 Add about half the reserved soaking liquid from the cèpes and the cream. Bring to the boil, stir in the cèpes and season well. Reduce the heat and simmer for about 5 minutes.

4 Cook the tortellini in boiling water according to the packet instructions until just tender.

Drain well. Toss with the sauce together with the chopped herbs and butter.

5 Divide the pasta between warmed plates and trickle over the truffle oil. Serve garnished with a few herb sprigs.

ingredients note

A tip about truffle oil – buy the most concentrated you can. It may be expensive, but the pronounced flavour makes such a difference to a dish.

serving note

Sometimes I serve this pasta dish with neat fillets of pan-fried red mullet on top.

Chicken, flageolet and fennel salad

This is a lovely summery dish for a buffet party or to eat on the patio. Flageolet beans are slim and an attractive green colour with a sweet, buttery flavour. Although popular in France, we don't use them often enough, so let's start to remedy that situation now. They are widely available in cans. Before using, simply rinse off the liquor gently under cold water, then drain in a colander.

serves 4

3 tbsp olive oil

3 fat garlic cloves, crushed

2 shallots, chopped

1 large fresh red chilli, deseeded and chopped

1 small bulb of fennel, chopped

2 x 400 g (14 oz) cans flageolet beans, rinsed and drained

grated zest and juice of 1 lemon

3 tbsp chopped mixed herbs, eg basil, parsley or mint

4 skinless, boneless chicken breasts, about 125 g (4½ oz) each

8 slices of pancetta

sea salt and freshly ground black pepper

1 Heat half the oil in a frying pan, add the garlic, shallots, chilli and fennel and sauté for about 5 minutes until softened.

2 Add the beans, lemon zest and juice and seasoning. Cook for 5 minutes, then stir in the herbs. Set aside.

3 Season the chicken well and drizzle over the remaining oil. Heat a separate frying pan or ridged griddle pan, add the chicken breasts and cook for about 5 minutes on each side until firm when pressed with the back of a fork. Season well during cooking.

4 Meanwhile, grill the pancetta until crisp, then snip into large pieces with kitchen scissors.

5 Divide the bean mixture between serving plates. Arrange the chicken breasts on top, then scatter over the pancetta and serve.

Don't be afraid of cooking a savoury dish with a sweet wine. It blends perfectly with the other flavours, and it's certainly a good talking point at the table. Here, a sweet-and-savoury risotto is matched with pan-fried chicken breasts. Buy the nicest corn-fed organic chicken you can for the best flavour. You'll need to make the Muscat and vanilla syrup, page 136, for this dish first, but it stores well for later use. You can, however, make the dish without it. A little basil oil is good for dressing the dish just before serving.

Chicken breasts with asparagus and muscat risotto

serves 4

25 g (1 oz) butter
2 tbsp olive oil
3–4 shallots, finely chopped
2 fat garlic cloves, crushed
200 g (7 oz) risotto rice (arborio or carnaroli)
100 ml (3½ fl oz) muscat wine, or another sweet dessert wine
700 ml–1 l (1¼–1¾ pts) fresh chicken stock (buy ready-made in a tub)
150 g (5½ oz) asparagus spears, stalks chopped and tips reserved

4 skinless, boneless chicken breasts, about 125 g (4½ oz) each
2 plum tomatoes, quartered, deseeded and finely chopped
2 tbsp chopped mixed fresh chervil and chives
2 tbsp Muscat and vanilla syrup (optional, *see* page 136)
1–2 tbsp mascarpone
basil oil, for drizzling
sprigs of fresh basil or parsley, to garnish
sea salt and freshly ground black pepper

1 Heat the butter with the half the oil in a saucepan, add the shallots and garlic and sauté gently for about 5 minutes until softened.

2 Stir in the rice and cook for 1–2 minutes until lightly toasted. Add the wine, bring to the boil, stirring, and cook for about 5 minutes until the liquid is absorbed, stirring frequently.

3 Heat the stock until simmering and add a quarter to the rice. Simmer, uncovered, until the stock is absorbed, stirring frequently. Add the chopped asparagus stalks with a ladleful of stock. Continue simmering, stirring occasionally, until the stock is absorbed. Add the remaining stock a ladleful at a time in the same way until all the stock is absorbed and the rice grains are plump and tender yet still retain a good 'bite'. This should take 15–18 minutes.

4 Meanwhile, about 10 minutes before the end of the cooking time for the risotto, heat a frying pan until you feel a good heat rising. Add the remaining oil, then the chicken breasts and sauté for about 3–5 minutes on each side, depending on their thickness. They should feel firm when pressed with the back of a fork. Season as they cook.

5 When the risotto is nearly ready, stir in the asparagus tips, chopped tomatoes, herbs, the Muscat and vanilla syrup, if using, and mascarpone. Mix well and cook gently for 2 minutes. Season to taste.

6 Divide the risotto between warmed serving plates. Slice each chicken breast into medallions and arrange on top of the risotto. Drizzle 1 tbsp of Muscat and vanilla syrup around each plate, if using, and trickle over a few drops of basil oil. Garnish with basil or parsley sprigs and serve.

Opinions differ about the origins of this hip classic. Some say it was a supper dish enjoyed by charcoal burners in Rome, other stories link it to American GIs in Italy at the end of the Second World War. Wherever it came from, a good carbonara needs crisp pancetta and matured fresh parmigiano reggiano, and is best freshly made in the pan. At all costs, avoid the glutinous sauces sold in jars under the same name.

Penne carbonara

serves 2 as a main course, 4 as a starter

250g (9oz) fresh or dried penne

2 tbsp olive oil

175g (6oz) pancetta, thinly sliced

5 free range egg yolks

150ml (¼ pt) double cream

100g (3½oz) parmesan, half finely grated, half as shavings

3–4 tbsp chopped fresh parsley

sea salt and freshly ground black pepper

1 Boil the penne in a large saucepan of lightly salted boiling water for about 8–10 minutes, or according to the packet instructions, until just tender. Rinse quickly under cold water to stop the cooking process.

2 Meanwhile, heat 1 tbsp of the oil in a frying pan, add the pancetta and fry until crisp.

3 In a large bowl, beat the egg yolks with the cream and grated Parmesan. Season well with pepper (hold back the salt until the end of the preparation); add the chopped parsley.

4 When the pasta is cooked, drain and toss immediately with the sauce in the bowl, together with the remaining oil and pancetta. Check the seasoning and serve in a warmed bowl. Top with shavings of parmesan.

Pesto pasta with picante chorizo and artichokes

There are a number of Spanish chorizo sausages now on sale, which make for good alfresco eating. My favourites are the large paprika-flavoured picante ones. Meaty and tasty, they are good cut into slices and quickly pan-fried ready to be tossed with pasta. This recipe works well with any pasta shapes.

serves 4

500 g (1 lb 2 oz) dried pasta shapes (any variety of a quality brand)

200 g (7 oz) picante chorizo, sliced

200 g (7 oz) jar artichoke hearts in oil, drained and oil reserved

3 tbsp freshly made pesto

50 g (1¾ oz) parmesan

sea salt flakes and freshly ground black pepper

1 Cook the pasta in a large saucepan of lightly salted boiling water, according to the packet instructions, until just tender. Drain, reserving a cup of the cooking water.

2 Meanwhile, heat a non-stick frying pan or a ridged griddle pan until you feel a good heat rising. Add the chorizo slices and cook for about 5 minutes, turning, until crisp on both sides.

3 Toss the pasta with the oil from the artichokes and season well. Cut the artichokes into wedges and add with the pesto to the chorizo in the pan to warm through. Toss the mixture in the pasta. If you like a slightly thinner sauce, add the cup of pasta cooking water.

4 Season the pasta and tip into a large warmed serving bowl. Shave the parmesan thinly using a swivel vegetable peeler and scatter over the pasta. Serve immediately.

Puddings and cakes

I love to finish a meal with a flourish, so puddings are very dear to my heart, and my stomach. They should be tempting and indulgent – after all, you don't *have* to eat them!

It's my experience when entertaining that people love to eat a well-executed version of a popular favourite. So if you've never made a real tiramisu, tried your hand at making ice-cream or want to make a deliciously different chocolate mousse, then simply sample the recipes in this chapter.

Puddings make great centrepieces for parties and special buffets, and offer the perfect excuse to show off your cooking skills. On this basis, I've included some glamorous, rather 'cheffy' dishes, such as a Summer fruit terrine (page 117) and Hot chocolate fondants (page 114). Others are quick yet impressive, such as Brandied roast figs (page 119) and Banana tarte tatin (page 112), which must rate as one of the quickest tarts ever.

I love baking, as a result of my country upbringing with a lovely Gran who let me 'help' her in the kitchen from a young age. One of the great pleasures home-baking brings is the sense of satisfaction you get when you pull out a perfect cake from the oven. The recipes I've included for biscuits, pastries and cakes are designed to make the most of the quality flours, sugars, dried fruits, spices, flower honeys and chocolates from the deli – all of which make a pronounced difference to the flavour and texture of the finished recipes.

Super-light pancakes

We don't make pancakes often enough in this country, which is a great shame when they make such good, quick hot desserts. I like to serve mine with fresh fruit – especially raspberries – ice-cream and some rich syrup trickled over – such as the Selsey Company's Vanilla Syrup. Alternatively, you could try light maple syrup.

**makes about
8 pancakes,
to serve 4**

175g (6oz) self-raising
flour
2 tsp baking powder
125g (4½oz) caster sugar
2 medium eggs
½–1 tsp vanilla essence
(optional)
250ml (9 floz) milk
softened butter or
sunflower oil, or both,
for cooking

1 Sift the flour and baking powder into a large bowl, stir in the sugar and make a well in the centre.

2 Break the eggs into a clean bowl and add the vanilla essence, if using, and 2 tbsp of the milk. Make a well in the dry ingredients and pour in the egg mixture. Using a whisk, gradually draw the dry ingredients into the egg mixture, add the remaining milk gradually as you whisk. Eventually, you should have a slightly lumpy batter. Don't over-mix the batter or it will make the pancakes heavy.

3 Heat a heavy based non-stick frying pan until you feel a good heat rising. Add a small knob of butter and/or trickle in a little oil. Spoon 2–3 tbsp of the batter into the pan. (If you want nice neat edges, you could stand a 8½cm (3¼in) round metal cutter in the pan to contain the batter. The resulting pancakes will resemble crumpets.)

4 Cook until bubbles rise to the surface and the batter becomes firm. Loosen from the bottom of the pan and flip over for a few seconds to brown the other side.

5 Repeat with the remaining batter, stacking the hot pancakes under a clean tea towel until ready to serve.

Chocolate and ginger cheesecake

This is possibly the quickest cheesecake in the world. It doesn't need any eggs and requires no cooking. I love entertaining at home, as you might have guessed! This was a quick dessert I devised on the spur of the moment for a three-course dinner when the guests were due any minute. You'll need two items from the sweet section of a deli. The cocoa powder should be the finest you can find – look out for those made by Charbonnel et Walker or the Chocolate Society. To add a spicy flavour, locate a small jar of preserved ginger in syrup – the type you buy in pretty Chinese jars at Christmas time. Serve with soft fruits.

serves 4–6

6 digestive biscuits, finely crushed

40 g (1½ oz) unsalted butter, melted

3 knobs of preserved stem ginger from a jar, plus 3 tbsp of the syrup

3 tbsp good-quality cocoa powder

grated zest and juice of 1 orange

4 tbsp double cream

4 tbsp icing sugar, sifted

300 g (10½ oz) mascarpone, softened

250 g (9 oz) fresh strawberries

sprigs of fresh mint, to decorate

1　Mix the crushed biscuits with the butter and 2 tbsp of the ginger syrup, then press into the base of a 18 cm (7 in) loose-based flan tin. Place in the freezer for a few minutes to set the crumbs.

2　Finely chop 2 of the knobs of ginger. Cut the remaining knob into fine strips and set aside.

3　Blend the cocoa powder with the orange juice, then beat in the orange zest, chopped ginger, cream and sugar. Gradually work the mascarpone into the mixture.

4　Spread the mixture on top of the biscuit base and place in the refrigerator for about 30 minutes to set.

5　To serve, push up the base of the flan tin carefully to unmould the cheesecake. Cut the cheesecake into wedges and arrange each wedge on a serving plate. Mix the ginger strips with the remaining ginger syrup. Divide the strawberries between the plates and trickle over the ginger sauce. Decorate each serving with a mint sprig and serve.

Hot walnut tart

This easy-to-prepare sweet flan combines bought pastry with a quick-mix filling. Check the use-by date if you are using a pack of shelled walnuts, since they will taste stale if they are ageing – not a problem you will encounter if you buy from a good deli, of course. One little tip – don't overcook the filling. It needs to be served a little gooey, so remove the flan tin from the oven when the mixture is still a little wobbly. Serve with scoops of caramel or toffee ice-cream, alternatively, try it with dollops of rich crème fraîche.

serves 6

350 g (12 oz) bought sweet shortcrust pastry, thawed if frozen

softened butter, for greasing (optional)

filling

250 g (9 oz) light soft brown sugar

225 g (8 oz) golden syrup

85 g (3 oz) butter

2 tbsp milk

1 tsp vanilla essence

4 large free-range eggs

300 g (10½ oz) walnuts, halved or chopped

1 Roll out the pastry on a lightly floured surface to fit a 23 cm (9 in) loose-based flan tin. If liked, you can lightly grease the flan tin first, but this is not necessary with most pastries. It does, however, make the pastry bake to a more golden colour.

2 Lay the pastry over the flan tin and press well into the base of the tin, bringing it up and over the sides. Leave untrimmed. Prick the base a few times with a fork and chill in the refrigerator for 30 minutes. Meanwhile, heat the oven to 190°C (375°F), Gas Mark 5.

3 Line the flan case with a large sheet of foil and baking beans, place on a baking sheet and bake 'blind' in the oven for 15 minutes.

4 Remove the foil and beans, trim the pastry edges with a sharp knife so that they are neat, then return the flan case to bake for a further 5 minutes. Leave to cool while you make the filling. Reduce the oven to 180°C (350°F), Gas Mark 4.

5 Heat the sugar, syrup and butter together in a saucepan until just blended, then remove from the heat and stir in the milk and vanilla. Leave to cool for 5 minutes, then beat the eggs and add to the syrupy liquid.

6 Scatter the nuts over the flan case and pour over the liquid filling. Return the flan to the oven and bake for 40–45 minutes until set but still a little soft in the centre – make sure that the top doesn't over-brown or burn. Remove from the oven and cool before pushing up the base of the flan tin to unmould the flan.

variation

You could use pecans in place of walnuts for a sweeter flavour.

Warm banana tarte tartin

This is a very quick and equally delicious tart. Use bananas that have spotty skins for the best flavour and serve with scoops of a good-quality ice-cream (see ingredients note).

serves 6–8

500 g (1 lb 2 oz) bought puff pastry, thawed if frozen

250 g (9 oz) caster sugar

25 g (1 oz) butter, softened

leaves stripped from 1 sprig of fresh rosemary, chopped

6 ripe bananas

1   Roll out the pastry on a lightly floured surface and cut into a 25 cm (10 in) round. Prick all over with a fork, then leave to rest in the refrigerator while you make the filling.

2   Place the sugar in a heavy-based saucepan and melt slowly over a very low heat until it turns a mid-caramel colour. You might like to add 1 tbsp of water to help it on its way, but most chefs don't. It is vital not to allow the syrup to bubble even around the edge until all the sugar grains have dissolved, otherwise the mixture will become grainy. It can help to brush the sides of the pan with a pastry brush dipped in cold water, to prevent any stray sugar grains from causing the syrup to crystallize.

3   As soon as the sugar turns a mid-caramel colour, plunge the pan base into a sink of cold water to halt the browning. It will spit alarmingly, so make sure that your arm is well covered. Beat in the butter until the mixture turns to a buttery caramel. Pour the caramel into an oven-proof frying pan, or 23 cm (9 in) shallow cake tin, turn and evenly coat the bottom and sides with the caramel.

4   Heat the oven to 190°C (375°F), Gas Mark 5. Sprinkle the chopped rosemary over the surface of the caramel, then slice the bananas on top. Finally, place the pastry round over the sliced bananas, pressing the edge down the sides of the filling all the way round.

5   Bake in the oven for 20–25 minutes until the pastry is crisp and golden. Remove carefully from the oven to prevent spilling the hot caramel. Allow to stand for a few minutes before carefully inverting on to a serving plate. Cut into wedges to serve.

ingredients note

For a really good bought ice-cream, I would recommend Rocombe Farm.

serving note

If you feel like making some ice-cream to serve with the tart, follow the recipe for Vanilla ice-cream, page 121, but replace one vanilla pod with one 10 cm (4 in) sprig of fresh rosemary.

Hot chocolate fondants

Hands up all those who love a dark and delicious hot chocolate soufflé? Almost everyone, I bet. Well, this recipe is sure to please. If you've ever wondered how chefs manage to bake a pudding with a rich sauce that oozes out, then follow these simple instructions. You can cook the mixture as soon as you've finished making it, but it also freezes brilliantly and can be baked once it has thawed.

serves 8

225 g (8 oz) dark chocolate with at least 60 per cent cocoa solids (*see* recipe introduction for Homemade florentines, page 123)

4 tbsp double cream

100 g (3½ oz) butter

35 g (1¼ oz) ground almonds

2 large eggs, separated

35 g (1¼ oz) cornflour

85 g (3 oz) caster sugar

1 Finely grate 40 g (1½ oz) of the chocolate and set aside. Gently melt a third of the remaining chocolate with the cream in a small saucepan, stirring well to mix. Remove and leave to cool.

2 Line a small plate with clingfilm and pour on the mixture. Place in the freezer for about 8 hours until set hard, then stamp out 8 small rounds using a 3 cm (1¼ in) round cutter. Set aside.

3 Melt half the butter and brush liberally all over the inside of 8 ramekins. Dust well with the grated chocolate, shaking out any excess. Set aside on a baking sheet.

4 Melt the remaining chocolate (including any shaken out excess) and butter in a small heatproof bowl over a pan of barely simmering water, or in a microwave-proof bowl in the microwave on Full for 2–3 minutes, stirring once. Do not overheat or the chocolate will 'seize', or turn solid. Scrape this mixture into

a bigger bowl, then beat in the ground almonds, egg yolks and cornflour.

5 Whisk the egg whites in a separate bowl until they form stiff but not dry peaks. Gradually beat in the caster sugar. You may like to use a hand-held electric whisk for this.

6 Fold the meringue mixture into the melted chocolate mixture. Spoon half the combined mixture into the base of the ramekins, place a chocolate disc on top, then fill each ramekin with the remaining mixture. Smooth the tops of the fondants and chill in the refrigerator while you heat the oven to 180°C (350°F), Gas Mark 4.

7 Bake the fondants in the oven for 10–15 minutes until risen and slightly wobbly, then remove and eat as soon as possible.

serving note

Serve with good-quality ice-cream – coconut-flavoured is especially good.

Tiramisu

There are numerous versions of this wickedly delicious Italian pud ranging from the simple to the ridiculous. This is my own variation on the theme, but I warn you it has quite kick since I use not only rum but also Tia Maria and the coffee liqueur, Kahlua. For best results, try and track down the Italian savoiardi or biscottine biscuits. They hold their texture well even when dipped in the coffee syrup.

serves 4–6

1 bourbon vanilla pod (*see* ingredients note) or 1 tsp vanilla essence

3 free-range egg yolks

50 g (1¾ oz) caster sugar

250 g (9 oz) mascarpone

250 ml (9 fl oz) double cream, lightly whipped

350 ml (12 fl oz) strong fresh coffee, cooled

2 tbsp rum

2 tbsp Kahlua

2 tbsp Tia Maria

about 300 g (10½ oz) savoiardi, biscottine or sponge fingers

2–3 tbsp cocoa powder, sifted

1 Slit the vanilla pod lengthways, if using, and scrape out the seeds with the tip of a knife.

2 Whisk the egg yolks and sugar with the vanilla seeds or essence until thick and creamy using a hand-held electric or rotary whisk. You can do this in a heatproof bowl set over a pan of gently simmering water for a thicker foam. The mixture is ready when a trail of foam forms as you lift up the beaters.

3 Remove from the heat, if using, and leave to cool, if necessary, whisking occasionally. Beat in the mascarpone, then fold in the whipped cream. Set aside.

4 Mix the coffee with the rum and liqueurs. Dunk the Italian biscuits or sponge fingers quickly into the coffee, making sure that they are completely immersed. If using sponge fingers, don't leave in the coffee for more than a second, or they will turn soggy. Arrange the biscuits or fingers in a layer in an attractive glass bowl and top with half the mascarpone and cream mixture.

5 Repeat with another layer of dunked biscuits or fingers and the remaining mascarpone and cream mixture. Shake the cocoa powder over the top in an even layer, then leave to set in the refrigerator for at least 2 hours.

safety note

This recipe contains raw egg yolks.

ingredients note

The best-quality vanilla pods come from Madagascar, and bourbon are the very best. Sold in vials, they are fatter and fuller than the ordinary variety, and better value.

Basil-scented summer fruit terrine with lime syrup

I really enjoy mixing and matching unusual combinations of herbs and fruits. The sweet aniseed-like flavour of fresh basil is wonderful with summer berries, and especially complements the flowery fragrance of a ripe mango. The lime syrup offers a refreshing tangy contrast. Consider how the terrine will look as you layer the fruits, and aim for a good contrast of colours. Try a random jumble of colour, like a modern splatter painting.

serves 6

6 leaves of gelatine
500ml (18 floz) water
200g (7oz) caster sugar
3 tbsp vodka
1 ripe mango
500g (1lb 2oz) strawberries
250g (9oz) raspberries
250g (9oz) blueberries
about 12 large basil leaves, plus extra for decoration

syrup

50g (1¾oz) caster sugar
grated zest and juice of 4 limes
150ml (¼pt) water
1 tbsp arrowroot

1 Line a 1kg (2lb 4oz) terrine mould or loaf tin with clingfilm, allowing an ample amount to fall over the sides. Slide the gelatine leaves into a bowl of cold water to soften.

2 Meanwhile, bring the 500ml (18floz) water to the boil in a saucepan and add the 200g (7oz) sugar. Stir until the sugar is dissolved. Pour away the water from the softened gelatine and lightly squeeze out any excess water. Slip the wet sheets into the hot sugar syrup and stir for a few seconds until dissolved. Add the vodka, then pour into a jug.

3 Peel and slice the mango into thin strips. Hull the strawberries and set aside any small dainty ones and some perfect raspberries for decorating. Slice the unreserved strawberries.

4 Half fill a large bowl (a washing-up bowl, for example) with very, very cold water and add as many ice cubes as you can find.

5 Pour a layer, about ½cm (¼in) deep, of the liquid jelly into the base of the terrine mould or loaf tin and place in the bowl of iced water. It should set quickly. Add a layer of fruits of your choice, then pour over a little more liquid jelly. Press down into the jelly any fruits that bob up to the surface. Again, allow

to set, then arrange a few basil leaves over the top. Continue adding layers of fruit, jelly and basil leaves in the same way.

6 When all the fruits are used up and neatly submerged in jelly, place the terrine in the refrigerator to chill completely, preferably overnight. (I place the terrine on a flat plate or tray so that it doesn't accidentally get knocked or disturbed.)

7 Meanwhile, to make the syrup, place the sugar, lime juice and water in a saucepan and bring to the boil. Mix the arrowroot with 1 tbsp cold water until clear. Whisk into the hot liquid in the pan until it thickens and becomes clear. Pour through a sieve to remove any arrowroot lumps. Stir in the lime zest and leave to cool, stirring occasionally.

8 To turn out the terrine, hold the tin over a wet oval serving platter or board and shake down firmly. The mould should slip out without the need to dip in hot water. Peel off the clingfilm. Cut the terrine into 2cm (¾in) slices and arrange on serving plates Drizzle around the lime syrup and decorate with the reserved strawberries, raspberries and extra basil leaves.

Saffron and honey pears

serves 8

2 good pinches
of saffron strands
1 lemon
1 orange
300g (10½oz)
caster sugar
500ml (18 floz) water
6 tbsp clear flower honey
8 slightly under-ripe
comice pears

This recipe has a wonderful medieval feeling to it and makes a lovely light dessert for the end of a rich dinner. Saffron may be the world's most expensive spice but it is also one of the most aromatic, and a little goes a very long way. Just a couple of pinches of the golden stamens give a good depth of flavour and colour. The best saffron comes from Spain. Stamens with a deep red colour have more flavour than yellow ones – a fact exploited by the cunning spice-producers who wrap the stamens in red transparent paper so that you can't tell the red from the yellow. Check the pack carefully before you buy. Choose a good honey for this recipe, too. My favourite brand, Viadiu, comes from Portugal in a number of different flower flavours.

1 Steep the saffron stands in 2 tbsp boiling water for 5 minutes.

2 Meanwhile, peel the zest from the lemon and orange in thin strips using a swivel vegetable peeler. Squeeze the juice from the lemon. Keep the orange for another use.

3 Place the zest in a large saucepan with the sugar and water. Bring slowly to the boil, stirring, until the sugar is dissolved. Reduce the heat and simmer gently for about 2–3 minutes. Add the saffron strands with its soaking water and the honey.

4 Peel the pears with a swivel vegetable peeler. Using the end of the peeler or the tip of a small sharp knife, remove the core from the base. Leave the stalks in place for decoration. Add the pears to the pan and bring to the boil. Reduce the heat, cover and simmer for about 30 minutes, turning the pears occasionally, until tender. To hold the pears under the syrup, wet a large sheet of greaseproof paper and crumple it, then press it down on the pears. Remove the pears with a slotted spoon and place in a large jar with a tight-fitting lid – Kilner-type jars are the best.

5 Boil the syrup for 10 minutes to thicken slightly and pour over the pears. Leave until quite cold before serving.

serving note

I serve these pears with a homemade crème brulée, but try a mixture of half mascarpone to half whipped double cream flavoured with vanilla-flavoured caster sugar (*see* ingredients note, page 119).

On one of my trips through Italy, I came across a wonderful old grandmother who cooked figs in a wood-burning oven, which she drizzled liberally with butter, sugar and brandy. Just as she was about to draw them from the oven, they caught fire and she simply blew out the flames without turning a hair. Alongside the figs on our plates she plopped spoonfuls of a crunchy, sweet-cream flavoured cream, with a cocktail of liqueurs and spirits, known as panna montata. This is my interpretation of her traditional recipe.

Brandied roast figs

serves 4

200 ml (7 floz) double cream

2 tbsp vanilla-flavoured caster sugar (*see* ingredients note)

2 tbsp granulated sugar

1 tbsp Cognac

1 tbsp Grand Marnier

1 tbsp kirsch

1 tbsp Brizard (apricot liqueur)

8 ripe figs, as large as you can find

40 g (1½oz) butter

4 tsp caster sugar

4 tsp brandy

1 To make the panna montata, whisk the cream until softly stiff, then fold in the vanilla and granulated sugars, followed by the 4 liqueurs. Scoop into a pretty serving bowl and chill in the refrigerator until required.

2 Heat the oven to 220°C (425°F), Gas Mark 7. Snip off the tops of the fig stalks, then cut the figs into quarters from the top to bottom but leaving the quarters attached at the base. Press your finger down through the centre of each fig to open up like a star. Place in a shallow heatproof dish.

3 Drop a small knob of the butter in the middle of each fig, then spoon in the caster sugar. Trickle over the brandy and place immediately in the oven. Leave for 6–8 minutes until golden brown with slightly charred tips. If they catch fire as you take them out of the oven, simply give them one big huff and puff and blow out the flames.

4 Leave to cool for a few minutes, then serve with the chilled panna montata.

ingredients note

You can buy vanilla sugar, but it costs a lot for what is essentially a very simple item. Just stick 2 or 3 vanilla pods in the centre of a bag or jar of sugar and you'll find that the flavour permeates through the sugar. The vanilla pods can be ones that have had their seeds removed for use in a previous dish.

Vanilla ice-cream with crushed meringues

makes about
1 l (1¾ pts)

2 bourbon vanilla pods
(*see* ingredients note,
page 115)
500 ml (18 fl oz) double
cream
150 ml (¼ pt) whole milk
175 g (6 oz) caster sugar
8 egg yolks
2 crushed meringue shells

If you find yourself with an under-used ice-cream maker, then you must try making your own fresh cream ice-cream. For best results you'll need one of those machines that has a mini built-in freezer unit that churns as it freezes. If not, a rotating machine that you place in the freezer would just about be acceptable. The addition of crushed meringues is the extra-special touch in this recipe. We sell Cotswold meringues – the greatest – in our deli, they are as good as homemade, light and crispy on the outside and gooey in the centre.

1 Using a sharp knife, slit the vanilla pods lengthways and scrape out the tiny seeds with the tip of the knife. Scrape the seeds into a saucepan with the cream and milk, then add the pods, too.

2 Stir in the sugar and bring the milk slowly to the bowl, stirring until the sugar is dissolved. Be careful not to let the milk boil over.

3 Place a bowl on a damp cloth to hold it steady, add the egg yolks and whisk until lightly frothy. Pour the scalded creamy milk on to the yolks in small amounts, whisking well until combined.

4 Return the mixture to the pan and stir over the lowest possible heat until it begins to coat the back of a wooden spoon and thickens slightly. Do not overheat or it will curdle.

5 Immediately strain through a fine sieve into a wide bowl and leave to cool, stirring once or twice to prevent a skin forming.

6 When cold, pour into an ice-cream maker and churn until the mixture becomes a firm slush. Remove and scoop into a bowl. Lightly fold in the crushed meringues and spoon into a freezerproof container.

7 Freeze the mixture until solid, then cover and store. Use within 2 weeks. Allow to soften for 10 minutes before scooping.

serving note

This ice-cream is mind-blowing with fresh strawberries, blueberries or raspberries, or a mixture of all three.

variations

Use 2 large sprigs of fresh rosemary or tarragon instead of the vanilla and serve the rosemary ice-cream with chopped banana, or the tarragon ice-cream with chopped apple.

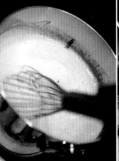

puddings and cakes

Honey mocha mousse

There seem to be a whole variety of different flavours in this seductively rich chocolate mousse, but believe me, they come together brilliantly. First, make sure you choose a good dark chocolate with at least 60 per cent cocoa solids (*see* the recipe introduction for Homemade florentines, page 123 and Introduction, page 11). To increase the chocolate flavour even further, choose a good-quality cocoa powder, like those from Charbonnel et Walker, the Chocolate Society, or the organic product from Green and Blacks. Also, make sure you use a good honey (*see* recipe introduction for Saffron and honey pears, page 118).

serves 4–6

150 g (5½oz) dark chocolate

50 g (1¾oz) cocoa powder, sifted

1 tbsp clear honey

2 tbsp orange liqueur, eg Grand Marnier or Mandarine

1 tbsp good-quality instant coffee

2 free-range large eggs, separated

25 g (1 oz) caster sugar

100 ml (3½ floz) double cream

1 Break up the chocolate and melt either in a heatproof bowl set over a pan of barely simmering water or in a microwave-proof bowl in the microwave on Full for 2–3 minutes, stirring once. Do not overheat or the chocolate will 'seize', or turn solid. Leave to cool slightly, then beat in the cocoa powder and honey.

2 Gently heat the liqueur in a small saucepan, add the coffee and stir until dissolved. Stir into the chocolate mixture. Leave to cool.

3 In a large bowl, whisk the egg yolks with the sugar until thick and creamy, and no longer grainy. This is best done with a hand-held electric whisk. With the beaters set on slow, gently whisk in the chocolate mixture.

4 In a separate bowl, whip the cream until softly stiff. Fold into the egg and chocolate mixture with a large metal spoon.

5 Place the egg whites in a large grease-free bowl and whisk them until they form soft peaks using clean, grease-free beaters. Fold the egg whites into the mousse mixture using a large metal spoon.

6 Divide the mousse between 4–6 pretty serving glass dishes or ramekins. Place in the refrigerator to chill for at least 1 hour, but they will keep overnight.

serving note

Serve with fresh raspberries and a ready-made raspberry coulis, or simply a trickle of single cream or runny half-fat crème fraîche.

safety note

This recipe contains raw eggs.

I regard florentines as the ultimate indulgence – all that lovely dried fruit in a chewy butterscotch base with a deliciously thick layer of chocolate underneath. The trouble is that bought florentines often fall down on the quality of the chocolate used. Since they are so easy to bake at home, take the opportunity to use the best chocolate available.

Chocolate is categorized according to the percentage of cocoa solids it contains, ranging from 30 per cent in milk chocolate at the bland end to more than 70 per cent at the other, bitter end of the scale (*see* Introduction, page 11). My advice here is to use a dark, relatively bitter variety, ie 60 per cent cocoa solids, to contrast with the cloyingly sweet biscuit base. I would recommend Valhrona, but there are other good brands around. Turn the pack over and check the labelling for the contents. Florentines can be made ahead and make great presents especially around Christmas time.

Homemade florentines

makes about 12

50 g (1¾ oz) French glacé cherries – natural-coloured variety are best

100 g (3½ oz) unsalted butter

125 g (4½ oz) caster or unrefined light soft brown sugar

3 tbsp double cream

150 g (5½ oz) flaked almonds, lightly crushed

2 tbsp chopped preserved stem ginger (optional)

25 g (1 oz) plain flour

225 g (8 oz) dark chocolate with about 60 per cent cocoa solids (*see* recipe introduction)

1 Chop the cherries into quarters, then rinse well in a sieve under tepid running water. Pat dry with kitchen paper and set aside. Heat the oven to 180°C (375°F), Gas Mark 4. Lightly grease 2 baking sheets.

2 Melt the butter in a saucepan, stir in the sugar and allow to bubble for 1 minute. Remove from the heat and stir in the cream, followed by the cherries, almonds, ginger (if using) and flour.

3 Drop spoonfuls, well spaced apart, on to the baking sheets; teaspoonfuls make dainty florentines, while dessertspoonfuls will create more generous ones – the choice is yours.

4 Bake in the oven for 5 minutes, then check to see if they need re-shaping with a palette knife into neat rounds. Return to the oven for another 4–5 minutes.

5 Leave for 1 minute to firm slightly before removing with a palette knife and transferring to a wire rack to crisp.

6 Meanwhile, break up the chocolate and place in a shallow heatproof or microwave-proof bowl. Melt either over a pan of barely simmering water or in the microwave on Full for about 2–3 minutes, stirring once. Do not overheat, since it will 'seize', or turn solid.

7 To coat the biscuits, either dip one side in the chocolate or simply spread with the melted chocolate using a palette knife. Make squiggly lines with a fork in the chocolate, if liked, and leave to set, chocolate side up, on the wire rack. The florentines will store in an airtight container for up to 2 weeks.

Panna cotta

The Italians certainly do have some lovely desserts, and this is one of them. It is a rich, creamy orange and vanilla jelly that you can make earlier in the day and serve chilled with a dish of spiced oranges (*see* recipe on page 126).

serves 8

2 oranges

1.2 l (2 pts) double cream

2 vanilla pods, slit lengthways and seeds removed, seeds and pods reserved

150 g (5½ oz) caster sugar

4 leaves gelatine or 1 sachet gelatine crystals

125 ml (4 fl oz) milk

5 tbsp vodka

1 Grate the zest of the oranges. Place in a deep non-stick saucepan with 800 ml (1 pt 7 fl oz) of the cream, the vanilla seeds and pods and the sugar. Bring to the boil, stirring once or twice, then reduce the heat and simmer until reduced by half. Stir frequently to prevent the bottom of the pan from burning. Remove from the heat.

2 If using gelatine leaves, place them in a bowl of cold water to soften. When softened, remove and set aside on a plate. Heat the milk until almost boiling, remove from the heat and add the soaked gelatine leaves. Stir until dissolved. If using gelatine crystals, sprinkle the crystals over the cold milk and allow to soak. Heat over a very low heat until dissolved, stirring once or twice.

3 Strain the milk through a sieve into the reduced cream mixture, stir and leave to cool. Discard the vanilla pods.

4 When the cream and gelatine mixture is cold but not quite set, whip the remaining cream and fold into the setting cream together with the vodka. Pour this mixture into a large wet mould of about 1 l (1¾ pt) capacity or 8 x 150 ml (¼ pt) moulds or ramekins. Place in the refrigerator until firmly set.

5 To serve, turn the panna cotta on to wet serving plates by running a knife round the edge.

serving note

Serve with spiced oranges and spun sugar. To prepare spun sugar: it is best to use a sugar thermometer for this technique. Place 250 g (9 oz) granulated sugar into a deep saucepan and heat gently until completely dissolved, stirring occasionally. When the mixture reaches 152°C (306°F), immediately remove from the heat and cool for 2 minutes. Rub a wooden rolling pin or steel rod lightly with sunflower oil. Dip a spoon into the syrup and quickly whirl it around the rolling pin. The syrup will form thin strands and will remain pliable for a few seconds so that you can slip it off and lightly shape it as desired.

Spiced oranges

This sweet and spicy orange accompaniment is simple to prepare and has the versatility to complement a wide range of sweet and savoury dishes. I highly recommend this served with the creamy Panna cotta, page 124.

serves 4–6

8 oranges
100 ml (3½ fl oz) water
100 g (3½ oz) caster sugar
1 cinnamon stick
3 large pinches of allspice

1 Remove the zest from 4 of the oranges using a swivel vegetable peeler and place in a large saucepan with the water, the sugar and spices. Bring to the boil, then reduce the heat and simmer for 15 minutes.

2 Meanwhile, cut away the white pith from all 8 fruits, then cut between the membranes to remove the segments, working over a bowl to catch the juice. Add the juice to the pan. Place the orange segments in a heatproof bowl.

3 Strain the contents of the pan over the orange segments and leave to cool. When cool, transfer to the refrigerator to chill.

Pineapple and polenta cakes with two coulis

Make a quick and easy cake mix using almonds and polenta for a nice crunchy texture, then bake on top of a rich butterscotch sauce in which you have sat pineapple rings. Serve with some delicious bought fruit sauces – apricot and raspberry coulis are two of my favourites.

serves 4–6

150g (5½oz) unsalted butter, softened

1–2 tbsp flour

175g (6oz) caster sugar

425g (15oz) can pineapple rings in natural juice, drained

100g (3½oz) ground almonds

75g (2½oz) fine polenta

½ tsp baking powder

a good pinch of salt

2 free-range medium eggs, beaten

grated zest and juice of 1 lemon

to serve

100ml (3½floz) ready-made raspberry coulis

100ml (3½floz) ready-made apricot coulis

1 Lightly grease 6 x 150ml (¼pt) ramekins with a little of the softened butter. Dust the sides with the flour and shake out the excess. Place the ramekins on a baking sheet.

2 Place 50g (1¾oz) of the sugar in a medium-sized heavy-based saucepan and add 1 tbsp water. Over a very low heat, melt the sugar to a caramel, shaking the pan occasionally. Do not allow it to bubble, even around the edge, until all the grains have dissolved. You may find it helpful to brush the sides of the pan with a pastry brush dipped in cold water, to prevent any stray sugar crystals from causing the syrup to crystallize.

3 When the sugar has dissolved, raise the heat and allow it to turn a light caramel colour. Using a long-handled wooden spoon, beat in a small knob of the remaining butter, taking care not to burn yourself. Immediately divide the caramel between the 6 prepared ramekins and set a pineapple slice on top.

4 Heat the oven to 180°C (350°F), Gas Mark 4. Mix together the almonds, polenta, baking powder and salt.

5 Beat the remaining butter and sugar together until light and creamy. Gradually beat in the eggs, followed by the dry almond and polenta mixture. Finally, beat in the lemon zest and juice.

6 Spoon the mixture into the ramekins over the top of the pineapple. Level the tops with the back of a teaspoon and bake in the oven for 15–20 minutes until risen and firm to touch.

7 Run a table knife around each ramekin and demould carefully on to serving plates. Take care that the hot caramel does not run out on to your hands. Trickle the raspberry and apricot coulis around each pudding.

serving note

Serve with cream or mascarpone on the side. Alternatively, thin the mascarpone with a little pouring cream, sweeten with a little sugar and add 1–2 drops vanilla essence.

Dripping cake

When I was a young lad, there always seemed to be pots of good country dripping in the kitchen. Beef and lamb fat were both added to the same pot ready to be spread on bread or toast to fill us up. My Gran, Marjorie, was the ultimate country cook – the type nostalgic films now feature in comforting soft focus. Except mine was for real. This is her favourite family cake which always seemed to be at hand whenever we wanted a hunk. It's what cookbooks would call a boiled fruit cake. Nowadays, not many of us have dripping pots, but you can still buy dripping. If it comes with a nourishing layer of meat jelly at the bottom, just scrape it off (save for adding to a stew) and use the clarified fat on top.

makes 1 x 15cm (6in) round cake

225g (8oz) mixed dried fruit (with candied peel included)

90g (3¼oz) clarified beef dripping

150g (5½oz) soft brown sugar

225ml (8 floz) water

225g (8oz) wholemeal flour

1 tsp baking powder

½ tsp bicarbonate of soda

a good pinch each of ground cinnamon, nutmeg and allspice

4 medium free-range eggs

1 Place the fruit, dripping, sugar and water in a saucepan and bring to the boil, stirring. Remove from the heat and leave to cool. (Gran would do this the night before.)

2 Heat the oven to 180°C (350°F), Gas Mark 4. Meanwhile, grease and line a deep round 15cm (6in) cake tin.

3 Sift the flour, baking powder, bicarbonate of soda and spices into a large bowl. Mix the fruit mixture into the dry ingredients with the eggs, beating well.

4 Tip the cake mixture into the prepared cake tin. Level the top and bake in the oven for about 1–1¼ hours until the top is golden brown and a clean metal skewer comes out clean when inserted into the centre of the cake.

5 Allow to cool in the tin for about 30 minutes, then turn out on to a wire rack and leave until cold. Peel off the lining paper and store in an airtight tin for up to 3 days.

serving note

There is only one true way to eat this cake – cut into slices and spread with lashings of butter and raspberry jam.

Quince and apple tarts with honey-walnut cream

These must rate as the fastest apple tarts this side of the Wild West, especially now that you can buy ready-rolled puff pastry. Use the Spanish membrillo quince paste or the Portuguese marmelo from a good deli, warming it gently if it is a little too thick to spread. The flavoured whipped cream is a good alternative to nutty ice-cream and melts divinely over the little tarts.

makes 4

2 x 375 g (13 oz) packs ready-rolled puff pastry, thawed if frozen

6 Golden Delicious or Granny Smith apples, cored

50 g (1¾ oz) butter, melted

125 g (4½ oz) membrillo or marmelo quince paste

25 g (1 oz) caster sugar

Honey-walnut cream

150 ml (¼ pt) double cream, whipped

2 tbsp clear honey

2 tbsp chopped walnuts

1 Cut 4 rounds from the 2 sheets of pastry about 15 cm (6 in) in diameter, using a small side plate or cake tin as a template. Place on 2 baking sheets, prick the bases well with a fork and chill in the refrigerator. Heat the oven to 200°C (400°F), Gas Mark 6.

2 Mix the whipped cream with the honey and nuts and chill in the refrigerator for about 30 minutes until firm.

3 Meanwhile, cut the apples in half lengthways and slice wafer thin. Brush the edges of the pastry rounds with a little melted butter. Spread the quince paste over the top of the rounds. Arrange the apple slices either in a neat fan shape or in a casual jumble on top. Brush the remaining melted butter on top and sprinkle over the sugar.

4 Bake in the oven for about 15–20 minutes until the pastry edges are crisp and golden brown. Slide the tarts off the baking sheets with a palette knife on to dessert plates. Scoop a smooth oval of honey-walnut cream using a dessert spoon dipped in hot water and place on a tart. Repeat for the other tarts and serve immediately.

Delis are often good sources of spices. Certainly, we stock a better range than the usual limited variety in supermarkets. Allspice, for example, is often not that easy to track down. Also known as Jamaica pepper or pimento, allspice is not another name for mixed spice but a distinct spice in its own right. It's just that our ancestors thought it smelt of all sorts of spices. You can buy the whole allspice berries (great for game stews, pâtés and rich cakes) or in ready-ground form. It is quite pungent, so a pinch is all you need. As with all spices, store them in a cool, dark cupboard rather than exposed on a kitchen shelf – spices lose their bouquet and colour in daylight. Remember to check their use-by dates regularly.

Spiced pear and apple danish

makes 6

375 g (13 oz) pack ready-rolled puff pastry, thawed if frozen

25 g (1 oz) unsalted butter

25 g (1 oz) caster sugar, or unrefined light soft brown sugar

1 large comice pear, peeled, cored and chopped

1 large golden delicious or granny smith apple, peeled, cored and chopped

a good pinch each of ground allspice and cinnamon

1 tsp chopped fresh rosemary leaves

1 egg yolk, beaten with a few drops water, for glazing

1 tbsp icing sugar

1 Cut the pastry sheet into 6 x 11 cm (4¼ in) squares. Make 4 x 4 cm (1½ in) cuts in each pastry square, 1.5 cm (⅝ in) from each outside edge. Prick the inner squares all over with a fork and place on a greased baking sheet. Chill in the refrigerator for 10 minutes.

2 Meanwhile, to make the filling, melt the butter with the sugar in a saucepan. Stir in the chopped fruit, spices and rosemary. Heat for just 2 minutes or so until slightly softened but not cooked. Remove from the heat and leave to cool. Heat the oven to 190°C (375°F), Gas Mark 5.

3 Divide the filling between the pastry squares, spooning it into the centre of each square. Draw the cut borders into the centre of each square and press together with a dab of the egg yolk glaze. Brush all the pastry with the glaze, then bake in the oven for 10 minutes. Remove the pastries from the oven and dust with the icing sugar, shaken from a sieve. Return to the oven to bake for a further 5–10 minutes when the sugar should start to caramelize.

4 Remove from the oven, and when the pastry is crisp, slide off on to a wire rack to cool.

Chutneys and preserves

T his small section is something of a 'potpourri' of recipes. It gathers together those extra touches that I use to add flavour interest to all kinds of foods. These include my special Muscat and vanilla syrup (page 136), perfect for pepping-up simple savoury dishes, and a Citrus and vanilla dressing (page 136) that works wonders for shellfish, along with my best-ever chutneys and relishes. All these items can be made ahead, then stored in the refrigerator or a cool larder, ready to be whipped out and added in dollops or dribbles whenever you want to make a dish truly memorable.

the deli cookbook

Plum chutney

makes about 350g (12oz), or enough for 1 medium jar

500g (1 lb 2oz) dark red plums
2 shallots, chopped
1 tbsp olive oil
100ml (3½ floz) white wine vinegar
3 tbsp water
1 cinnamon stick
100g (3½oz) demerara sugar

When I was running the kitchens at the Hotel du Vin in Winchester, after service when everyone else had packed up and gone home, my sous chef Chris and I would often work into the wee small hours, making up new dishes or practising adaptations of old ones. For some reason, that's when our creative spirits ran free. This 15-minute chutney was one of those ideas, which I like to make up in bulk to keep on hand (it keeps for up to two weeks in the fridge). It goes well with pan-fried halibut steaks (*see* page 54).

1 Cut the plums in half down the crease, twist the halves in opposite directions and pull apart. Prise out the stones and discard. Roughly chop the flesh.

2 Place the chopped shallots in a heavy-based saucepan with the oil and heat until sizzling. Sauté gently for 5 minutes until softened.

3 Add the plums, vinegar, water, cinnamon and sugar. Stir until the sugar is dissolved, then simmer for about 15 minutes, stirring occasionally, until softened and slightly thickened.

4 Meanwhile, heat the oven to 100–120°C (212–250°F), Gas Mark ½. Place a clean jam jar in the oven to warm. When the plum chutney is ready, spoon it into the jar. Seal with a lid and leave to cool completely.

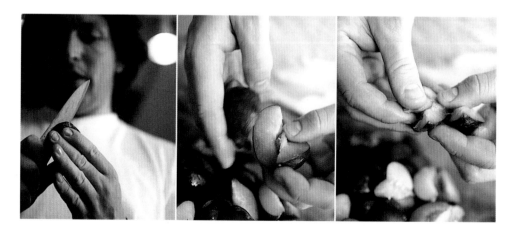

Muscat and vanilla syrup

**makes about
350ml (12 floz)**

700ml (1¼ pts) muscat
wine, or another sweet,
dessert wine

4 shallots, chopped

1 fat garlic clove,
roughly chopped

1 vanilla pod, split
in half lengthways
(*see* recipe introduction)

2 tsp coriander seeds,
roughly crushed

150ml (¼ pt) clear honey

This is a great flavouring syrup that takes very little time to
prepare. I store mine in a squeezy bottle – the type you find
on the tables of roadside 'caffs'. Actually, you can now buy these
(new and empty) from catering equipment stores. It is suitable
for all sorts of dishes, such as the Chicken breasts with asparagus
and muscat risotto, page 102, or try it trickled over cod and mash.
Make sure you buy fresh vanilla pods that are shiny and waxy
rather than dried and shrivelled, and ideally the bourbon variety
from Madagascar (*see* ingredients note, page 115).

Place all the ingredients in a wide saucepan. Bring to the boil, then
reduce the heat and cook on a medium simmer for about 20 minutes
until reduced by half. Leave to cool to room temperature, then strain
and pour into a bottle. Seal and store, but not in the fridge as it will turn
hard. It will keep for several weeks.

Citrus and vanilla dressing

**makes about
300ml (½ pt)**

grated zest and juice
of 1 lemon

grated zest and juice
of ½ orange

4 tbsp rice wine vinegar

150ml (¼ pt) olive oil

2 vanilla pods,
split lengthways

¼–½ tsp sea salt

freshly ground black
pepper, to taste

This dressing is delicious for shellfish, such as the Lobster,
mango and rocket tarts, page 28, or try it with pan-fried scallops,
chicken or salmon. Make sure you use fresh vanilla pods that
still have a lovely waxy feel to them. This is a good use for pods
whose seeds you have already used. Store the dressing in
a screw-top jar in the refrigerator.

Place all the ingredients in a screw-top jar – you may have to bend
the pods to fit. Screw on the lid and shake to emulsify. Store in
the refrigerator until required – it will keep for up to 2 weeks.

Cucumber and green pepper relish

This is similar to a fresh Mexican salsa. It simply involves finely chopping all the ingredients, mixing them together and leaving to marinate for half on hour or so. It's best to chop by hand – if you use a food processor you could end up with a sloppy mixture.

**makes enough
to serve 6–8**

½ large cucumber

2 red onions

2 green peppers, cored
and deseeded

6 ripe plum tomatoes

2 fat garlic cloves,
crushed

grated zest and juice
of 3 limes

4 tbsp olive oil

2 tbsp chopped
fresh coriander

sea salt and freshly
ground black pepper

1 Halve the cucumber lengthways, scoop out the seeds with a teaspoon, then finely chop the flesh. Place in a large bowl.

2 Finely chop the onions, peppers and tomatoes. Add to the bowl with the crushed garlic, lime zest and juice, oil, coriander, about 1 tsp salt and black pepper to taste.

3 Mix everything together well, then cover and chill in the refrigerator for 1 hour.

serving note

This fresh relish is ideal for serving with all sorts of grills, roasts and barbecued foods. It's also good as an accompaniment for curries.

Chicory and orange jam

This is my all-time favourite relish, which I make in batches ready to liven-up quick pan-fries. It goes really well with thick king scallops or plump free-range chicken breasts.

makes enough for 1 large jar

1 onion, chopped
1 fat garlic clove, chopped
25 g (1 oz) butter
1 tbsp olive oil
5 heads of fresh chicory, thinly sliced
peel and juice of 2 oranges
2 sprigs of fresh thyme
75 g (2½oz) caster sugar
250 ml (9 fl oz) dry white wine

1 Place the onion, garlic, butter and oil in a large heavy-based saucepan and heat until it starts to sizzle. Gently sauté the ingredients for about 5 minutes until softened.

2 Add the remaining ingredients and bring to the boil, stirring. Reduce the heat and simmer gently, uncovered, for 30–40 minutes until the chicory becomes transparent and wilted right down.

3 Meanwhile, heat the oven to 120°C (250°F), Gas Mark ½. Place a clean jam jar in the oven to warm. Once cooked, leave the jam to cool slightly before spooning into the warmed jam jar. Seal immediately and leave to cool completely. Use within 1 month.

chutneys and preserves

Menu combinations

Planning a meal that has a careful balance of flavours and textures can be tricky. Even when you think you know all the rules things can still go wrong. It's annoying to finish cooking and only then realise that the courses are all the same colour or that a smooth-textured paté is followed by a chicken mousse. Here are some useful guidelines to help you avoid the most common pitfalls.

Colour contrast

Think about the colours of each dish. In the main they should all be different, unless of course you are following a single colour theme, such as yellow/gold for a party. For instance, a tomato salad followed by a red curry would not be quite so appealing as a starter on a bed of green salad leaves.

Balancing flavours

Consider the strength of flavours in your meal – you don't want a spicy starter with a pungent main course; even Indian meals have a carefully thought out balance of spiciness. A piquant starter is often good to freshen your palate if you intend serving a creamy main dish.

Ingredient combinations

Where possible, contrast the main ingredient of the starter with that of the main course. Try not to have two meat or two fish dishes in the same meal, unless they are quite different from each other. For instance, salami followed by grilled chicken is fine but not a rich beef casserole.

Hot and cold

A cold main course is often best preceded by a hot starter, or a hot main course by a cold starter. But two cold dishes in a meal can work really well as long as they are sufficiently contrasted in both taste and texture.

Richness and light

Don't serve a series of rich dishes, for example a paté followed by a heavy roast with all the trimmings and then a chocolate mousse. The exception to this rule is at Christmas, when we expect to feel really full after the meal!

Recipe combinations from the book

Here are some two-course suggestions for dinner party menus. Choose whichever pudding you think your guests will enjoy most – but try to avoid serving a rich dessert after a heavy starter and main course. Also remember that a selection of fresh fruits or cheeses makes a simple and delicious alternative to the puddings in this book.

A salad of red peppers and olives, page 18
Cheats' coq au vin, page 56

Chilli garlic dressed mushrooms, page 16
Roast pork with balsamic butter bean broth, page 64

Bresaola with confit lemon rind and rocket salad, page 37
Pepper-crusted monkfish with mustard dill sauce, page 45

Scallop salad with salted capers and crispy sage, page 24
Loins of lamb with cumin and almond-dressed artichokes, page 62

Iberico ham with a herby leaf salad, page 34
Sea bass with summer herbs and roasted limes, page 40
New potato salad with truffle cream dressing, page 74

Salad of two smoked fish, page 25
Anchovy and garlic-studded roast lamb, page 63

Brandade of salt cod, page 21
Beef steaks with sun-blushed tomatoes and parsley, page 67

Hot onion bread with garlic and hand-peeled tomatoes, page 17
Pan-fried chicken with chilli beans, fennel and pancetta, page 58

Griddled asparagus with roasted red peppers, page 14
Salmon with wild garlic sauce and champ, page 50

Gedi goats' cheese bruschetta with quince and parma ham, page 31
Warm banana tarte tatin, page 112

Crispy speck, artichoke and black pudding salad, page 35
Pan-fried cod with vanilla shrimp butter, page 55

Salad of two smoked fish, page 25
Calves liver with port-flavoured pan juices, page 66

Index

A

anchovy and rosemary pizzas, 88

apples:

    spiced pear and apple Danish, 131

asparagus:

    chicken breasts with asparagus
        and Muscat risotto, 102

    griddled asparagus with roasted
        red peppers, 14

aubergine and mozzarella stack, 87

B

bacon *see* pancetta; speck

banana tarte tatin, 112

beef:

    beef steaks with sun-blushed
        tomatoes and parsley, 67

    bruschetta of smoked beef and
        melted brie, 36

    caramelized braised beef, 69

beetroot, caramelized, 74

brandade of salt cod, 21

brandied roast figs, 119

bread:

    hot onion bread with garlic and hand-
        peeled tomatoes, 17

    olive focaccia with rosemary oil, 76

    poppy seed snaps, 18

    roasted garlic and olive oil bread, 78

    smoked salmon and basil bread, 83

bresaola with confit lemon rind and
    rocket salad, 37

brill with Chinese lardons and green leaves, 51

bruschetta:

    Gedi goat's cheese, 31

    smoked beef and melted brie, 36

bubble and squeak cakes, 82

butter beans:

    butter bean and rosemary purée, 75

    roast pork with balsamic butter bean
        broth, 64

    butternut squash roasted with lemon
        and mustard, 79

C

cabbage:

    bubble and squeak cakes, 82

cakes:

    dripping cake, 129

    pineapple and polenta cakes, 127

calves liver with port-flavoured pan juices, 66

caramelized beetroot, 74

caramelized braised beef, 69

celeriac:

    celeriac remoulade, 72

    roast celeriac with vanilla and garlic, 72

cheat's coq au vin, 56

cheese, 9-10

    aubergine and mozzarella stack, 87

    bruschetta of smoked beef and melted
        brie, 36

    chargrilled vegetables with olives and
        goat's cheese, 16

    figs roasted with blue cheese and
        prosciutto, 32

    Gedi goat's cheese bruschetta, 31

    marinated mozzarella with red onion
        and spinach, 17

    Picos blue and caramelized onion tarts, 20

cheesecake, chocolate and ginger, 110

chicken:

    cheat's coq au vin, 56

    chicken breasts with asparagus and
        Muscat risotto, 102

    chicken, flageolet and fennel salad, 101

    pan-fried chicken with chilli bean, fennel
        and pancetta, 58

chicory and orange jam, 139

chilli garlic dressed mushrooms, 16

chocolate, 11

    chocolate and ginger cheesecake, 110

    honey mocha mousse, 122

    hot chocolate fondants, 114

chorizo:

    pesto pasta with picante chorizo
        and artichokes, 104

chutneys, 11

    plum chutney, 134

citrus and vanilla dressing, 136

cod, pan-fried with vanilla shrimp butter, 55

coffee:

    honey mocha mousse, 122

    tiramisu, 115

coq au vin, cheat's, 56

crab cakes, 94

cream: panna cotta, 12

cucumber and green pepper relish, 137

D

dressings, 11

    citrus and vanilla, 136

dripping cake, 129

duck:

    duck breasts with fennel paté
        and apples, 59

    honeyed duck confit with crispy seaweed
and creamy mash, 61

E

eggs:

    penne carbonara, 103

F

fennel:

    duck breasts with fennel paté
        and apples, 59

figs:

    brandied roast figs, 119

    figs roasted with blue cheese
        and prosciutto, 32

flageolet beans:

    chicken, flageolet and fennel salad, 101

    Florentines, homemade, 123

    focaccia, olive with rosemary oil, 76

fruit:

    basil-scented summer fruit terrine, 117

G

garlic:

    roasted garlic and olive oil bread, 78

Gedi goat's cheese bruschetta, 31

gnocchi:

grilled gravadlax with pesto gnocchi, 88

goat's cheese:

chargrilled vegetables with olives and
goat's cheese, 16

Gedi goat's cheese bruschetta, 31

gravadlax grilled with pesto gnocchi, 88

H

halibut:

charred smoked halibut and saffron
risotto, 98

halibut parcels with capers and
Pernod, 52

halibut steaks with beansprout and
coriander salad, 54

ham, 8

Iberico ham with a herby leaf salad, 34

herbs:

fresh leaf pasta, 81

honey:

honey mocha mousse, 122

honeyed duck confit with crispy seaweed
and creamy mash, 61

I

Iberico ham with a herby leaf salad, 34

ice-cream:

vanilla ice-cream with crushed
meringues, 121

L

lamb:

anchovy and garlic-studded
roast lamb, 63

loins of lamb with cumin and almond-
dressed artichokes, 62

leek and haddock risotto, 95

liver:

calves liver with port-flavoured
pan juices, 66

lobster, mango and rocket tarts, 28

M

meats, cold, 8-9

meringues:

vanilla ice-cream with crushed
meringues, 121

monkfish, pepper-crusted, with mustard
dill sauce, 45

mousse, honey mocha, 122

mullet on smoky red pepper salad, 91

muscat and vanilla syrup, 136

mushrooms: chilli garlic dressed
mushrooms, 16

tortellini in a cépes sauce, 99

mussel and artichoke
risotto, 90

N

noodles:

Thai prawn and noodle soup, 23

O

oils, 9-10

olive focaccia with rosemary oil, 76

olive oil, 9-10

onions:

marinated mozzarella with red
onion and spinach, 17

Picos blue and caramelized onion
tarts, 20

red onion and créme frêche
pizza, 86

oranges:

chicory and orange jam, 139

panna cotta, 124

spiced oranges, 126

P

pak choi:

brill with Chinese lardons and
green leaves, 51

pancakes, super-light, 108

pancetta:

penne carbonara, 103

panna cotta, 124

pasta:

fresh leaf pasta, 81

lemon-dressed pasta with chargrilled
salmon, 96

penne carbonara, 103

pesto pasta with picante chorizo and
artichokes, 104

tortellini in a cépes sauce, 99

pastries:

spiced pear and apple Danish, 131

pears:

saffron and honey pears, 118

spiced pear and apple Danish, 131

penne carbonara, 103

peppers:

griddled asparagus with roasted red
peppers, 14

mullet on smoky red pepper salad, 91

salad of roasted peppers and olives, 18

pesto:

grilled gravadlax with pesto
gnocchi, 88

pesto pasta with picante chorizo
and artichokes, 104

pickles, 11

Picos blue and caramelized onion tarts, 20

pineapple and polenta cakes, 127

pizzas:

anchovy and rosemary pizzas, 88

red onion and créme frêche pizza, 86

plum chutney, 134

polenta:

pineapple and polenta cakes, 127

poppy seed snaps, 18

pork: roast pork with balsamic butter
bean broth, 64

potatoes:

bubble and squeak cakes, 82

new potato salad with truffle cream
dressing, 74

potato, truffle and Parma ham terrine, 30

prawn and noodle soup, Thai, 23

Q

Quince and apple tarts, 130

R

relishes:
    chicory and orange jam, 139
    cucumber and green pepper relish, 137
risotto:
    charred smoked halibut
    and saffron risotto, 98
    chicken breasts with asparagus and
    muscat risotto, 102
    leek and haddock risotto, 95
    mussel and artichoke risotto, 90
rocket:
    bresaola with confit lemon rind
    and rocket salad, 37

S

saffron and honey pears, 118
salads:
    bresaola with confit lemon rind
    and rocket salad, 37
    celeriac remoulade, 72
    chicken, flageolet and fennel salad, 101
    crispy speck, artichoke and black
    pudding salad, 35
    halibut steaks with beansprout and
    coriander salad, 54
    Iberico ham with a herby leaf salad, 34
    mullet on smoky red pepper salad, 91
    new potato salad with truffle cream
    dressing, 74
    roasted peppers and olives, 18

salad of two smoked fish, 25
scallop salad with salted capers
and crispy sage, 24
sea bass with sprouting wheatgerm
salad, 43
salami, 8
salmon:
    lemon-dressed pasta with
chargrilled salmon, 96
    salmon with red onion pickle, 48
    salmon with wild garlic sauce
    and champ, 50
salt cod, brandade of, 21
sausages, blood, 9
scallop salad with salted capers
    and crispy sage, 24
sea bass:
    sea bass with pinenuts, artichokes
    and tomatoes, 42
    sea bass with sprouting wheatgerm
    salad, 43
    sea bass with summer herbs, 40
seafood pot, 93
smoked eel: salad of two smoked fish, 25
smoked haddock:
    leek and haddock
    risotto, 95
smoked salmon and basil bread, 83
smoked trout:
    salad of two smoked fish, 25
soup, Thai prawn and noodle, 23
speck, 8-9
crispy speck, artichoke and black pudding
    salad, 35

squash:
    butternut squash roasted with
    lemon and mustard, 79
syrup, muscat and vanilla, 136

T

tarts: hot walnut tart, 111
    lobster, mango and rocket tarts, 28
    Picos blue and caramelized onion
    tarts, 20
    quince and apple tarts, 130
    warm banana tarte tatin, 112
terrines: basil-scented summer fruit
    terrine, 117
    potato, truffle and Parma ham terrine, 30
Thai prawn and noodle soup, 23
tiramisu, 115
tomatoes: hot onion bread with garlic and
    hand-peeled tomatoes, 17
tortellini in a cépes sauce, 99
tuna: basil oil tuna with deep-fried garlic, 27
    seared tuna with quinoa and kalamata
    olives, 46
turbot with boudin and black-eye beans, 47

V

vegetables: chargrilled vegetables with olives
    and goat's cheese, 16
vinegars, 10-11

W

walnut tart, 111

Photographic acknowledgements James Martin and the staff at Mitchell Beazley would like to thank Horwood Homewares (tel 0117 940 0000) for supplying Stellar stainless steel saucepans and kitchen equipment, Kenwood UK (tel 0239 247 6000) for supplying a Kenwood Chef, Magimix UK Ltd (tel 01483 427411) for supplying an ice-cream maker, The Conran Shop (tel 020 7589 7401) and David Mellor (tel 020 7730 4259) for supplying china, cutlery and glasses

the deli cookbook